MacOS Big Sur For Seniors

A RIDICULOUSLY SIMPLE GUIDE TO USING MACOS 11 FOR MACBOOKS AND IMACS

SCOTT LA COUNTE

RIDICULOUSLY SIMPLE BOOKS

ANAHEIM, CALIFORNIA

www.RidiculouslySimpleBooks.com

Table of Contents

Disclaimer: *Please note, while every effort has been made to ensure accuracy, this book is not endorsed by Apple, Inc. and should be considered unofficial.*

INTRODUCTION

Switching from Windows to Mac? Let's make this as easy as possible!

Big Sur adds some powerful new features to macOS, which is fantastic news...if you know how to use them.

If you're like many adults, however, then your first computer was probably a Windows computer—or maybe it only had a command interface. For most of us, macOS is something a little new.

MacOS isn't complicated but switching from another operating system can be a little confusing at first. This guide is intended to help you make the switch.

In addition to showing you how exactly it works, it walks you through how you can still do all those Windows things you have grown to love.

This book is intended for people who want to get started quickly with the OS. For that reason, it's not as comprehensive as other guides. It covers the most popular features, but not how to do configurations you probably have never heard of and will never want to do.

I purposely have done my best to make this handbook a little more casual and fun than what you expect from most macOS manuals. MacOS is a fun operating system, and any guide you read should be an equally fun read.

Some of the covered features include:

- What's new to macOS Big Sur
- How you do all those Windows "things" on a Mac
- Apple Services (Apple Music, Apple News, iCloud, Apple Card, Apple Arcade, Apple TV+)
- Using Siri
- How to find things / how to organize things to make them easy to find
- Setting up Internet and Email
- Using Sidecar
- Using Control Center
- Using Time Machine
- Parental Controls
- Downloading / Updating apps
- Organizing photos
- Using Safari
- Protecting your privacy
- Managing your passwords
- Using Maps
- Making phone calls
- Sending, replying, and pinning messages

- Multitasking
- And much, much more!

Are you ready to start enjoying the new macOS? Then let's get started!

Note: this book is based off of MacOS Big Sur: Getting Started with MacOS 11 for MacBooks and iMacs but has expanded discussion of accessibility features. It is not endorsed by Apple, Inc. and should be considered unofficial.

[1]

What's So Great About Mac?

This chapter will cover:

- What's so great about Macs
- Are they really virus free?
- OS without the bloat
- A look at the hardware

Before diving into the actual software, let's address the obvious: why pick Mac?

I was in the Windows camp for a long time; I'd see the Mac and think it was just a computer for hipsters. Sure they were nice to look at—they were shiny and didn't look plastic-y and cheap…but they were also expensive.

But then I actually used one, and I was blown away. Here's why…

Fewer Viruses

You've probably heard someone say they use a Mac because they don't get viruses. That's not true. Any computer can get a virus. But it is true that Macs are generally less prone to viruses and are more secure.

The reason you don't hear about Mac viruses very often is twofold:

1. While it's hard to pinpoint just how many computers there are in the world, most computers are still Windows. So, if you are a hacker wanting to wreak havoc into cyberspace, then your obvious target would be the one with the largest audience.
2. The second reason is MacOS is built by Apple, for Apple. Windows builds their OS to be built for essentially any computer, which opens the door for vulnerabilities.

I know a lot of Mac users and rarely do I hear someone say they have a virus. If you are concerned, however, one popular free virus protector is called Bitdefender Virus Scanner (http://www.bitdefender.com/).

Keeping It Simple

When it comes to design, Apple likes to make things that are beautiful and simple. This philosophy can be seen in their watches, iPhones, and iPads—across all their products.

Because Apple spends so much time keeping it simple, you also have seen the last days of computer crashes and blue screens of deaths.

Apple spends a lot of time thinking not just about what the computer should do, but how people will do it. If you've been using Windows all of your life, then all the different menus and buttons might seem intimidating at first—but don't stress! This book will show you how much easier it actually is.

If you have any other Apple products, then many of the common Mac tasks will probably seem very similar to you. What's more, if you have an iPhone, iPad, or even Apple TV, then they all work and interact with each other.

No Bloat

I remember my last Windows computer. I couldn't wait to turn it on...and then I couldn't wait to turn it off! Your first hour should be spent just having fun exploring it, but my first hour was spent uninstalling programs!

One reason Windows computers are cheaper is that manufacturers team up with software companies and install all kinds of unnecessary programs—most of them are just free trials.

With Mac, you turn your computer on for the first time, create an ID if you don't already have one, put in your Wi-Fi, and log in to iTunes / iCloud. That's it. It should take less than ten minutes to get your computer up and running once you get it out of the box.

A Look At the Hardware

In 2008, the MacBook Air was revolutionary. It was powerful, and yet thin enough to fit in an envelope! Years past, and it became a little less revolutionary. Other computers were just as thin, but even more powerful.

The 2018 model, however, put MacBook Air back in the spotlight with a new model that had a Retina display (older models did not), fingerprint sensor, and power that was almost equal to MacBook Pros.

There aren't a lot of pots on MacBook Air's. One side is two Thunderbolt 3 / USB-c ports (this is where your power will plug in as well); USB-c is the new standard of USB and lets you transfer data at a much faster rate. If you still need regular adapters you can buy them cheap; you can also buy USB drives with both USB and USB-c connections.

The reverse side has a headphone jack; MacBook Airs have Bluetooth, so you can also listen to music with a wireless headphone—or you can use the computers built-in speakers.

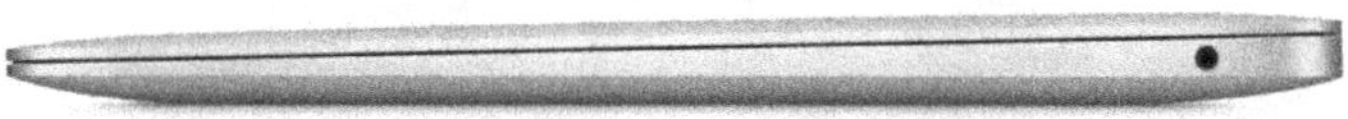

MacBook Pro vs. MacBook Air

MacBook Air's used to be the lightest notebook in Apple's lineup; they still are. But MacBook Pros are only slightly heavier. So, weight is no longer the deciding factor for most people.

What's right for you? If you absolutely must have Gold as a color, then the Air is your only choice, as it's the only one with this color.

Air's also only come in one screen size; if you want a larger screen, then Pro's are your only option.

The processors on the Pro and Air are comparable, but the Pro is slightly faster; the Pro also can be configured higher—meaning you can upgrade it to higher standards. The Pro's also have the edge on graphic cards, but the Airs still have very good cards. Airs can only be upgraded to 16GB of RAM; the 15 inch Pro (not the 13 inch) can be upgraded to 32GB

Battery-wise, the Airs get 12 hours vs the 10 hours on a Pro.

Pro's are currently the only notebooks that have the Touch Bar on the keyboard.

Finally, Pros have two additional USB-c ports.

[2] Switching From Windows

This chapter will cover:

- How to use Windows OS features on MacOS
- Transferring docs
- Compatibility
- Setup Assistant

So exactly how is Mac different from Windows? Throughout the book, I'll be making comparisons to help you, but first I want to give a rundown of some of the major differences.

Right Click

Right-clicking is probably second nature to you if you are a Windows user; on the Mac, it's all about gestures—touching the Trackpad (Mac's mouse) a certain way (or on new Macs, using more or less pressure) will bring up different options and menus.

As weird as it sounds, the first time I used a Mac, the right-click (or lack thereof) drove me crazy…until I figured out that right-clicking was actually there. To right-click on a Mac, click with two fingers instead of one. Alternatively, you can press Control and click with one finger.

If you have an old Windows USB mouse, you don't have to toss it—you can plug it into your Mac and it will work with no installation. The right-click will even work.

I'll explain how to customize your Trackpad later in the book, but if you'd like to jump ahead, you can go to System Preferences > Trackpad.

And don't worry about messing something up; it's very hard to harm a Mac!

Keyboard Shortcuts

This section will give you a very quick rundown of the more popular keyboard shortcuts; for a more detailed list, see Appendix A at the end of this book.

On a Windows computer, you might be used to using Control (CTRL) frequently; Control is on the Mac keyboard, but don't get confused—on a Mac, the Control button equivalent is the Command (⌘) Key (to the right of the keyboard). The good news is the letter combination for the most frequently used Windows shortcuts is almost always the same on a Mac—Control-C to copy is Command-C on the Mac; Control-X to Cut is Command-X; Control-V to Paste is Command-V.

On a Windows computer, you can hold Alt and Tab to cycle through programs...on a Mac you use Command and Tab.

The two most frequently used function keys (the buttons above the numbers) are F3 and F4; F3 will show a list of the programs you have open, and F4 brings up your Launchpad (all of your available programs...kind of like the Start menu on Windows).

Just keep reminding yourself that while it looks different, it's really not...Windows has File Explorer, Mac has Finder; Windows has the Start Menu, Mac has Launchpad; Windows has the Ribbon menu, Mac has the Top Navigation menu.

Below is a quick overview of what things are called on Windows and what they are called on a Mac:

Windows	Mac

Windows Explorer / My Computer / Computer	Finder
Control Panel	System Preferences
Programs	Applications (often shortened to apps)
Task Bar and Start Menu	Dock
Tray	Menulets
Recycle Bin	Trash
Task Manager	Activity Monitor
Media Center	iTunes

Transferring Documents

The thing a lot of people worry about when updating any computer is how to get all of your information from your old computer to your new computer. With Macs, it's a pretty simple task—you can even take it into your local Apple Store for free help (appointments are needed, so don't just walk in).

If you don't want to wait for an appointment or you just like doing things on your own, there's already a tool on your computer to help: it's called Migration Assistant. Be advised, you do need an Internet connection.

To start, go to your Windows computer and either search any search engine for "Windows Migration Assistant" or go directly to https://support.apple.com/kb/DL1557?locale=en_

US. Once you are there, download and install the program on your Windows computer.

From your Mac, click the Launchpad icon (i.e. the rocket on your taskbar).

Next, click on Other and then click Migration Assistant.

To use Migration Assistant, everything that is open on your Mac will be closed, so make sure and save your work, and don't start until you are ready.

From the setup, click Continue, and then select "From another Mac, PC, Time Machine backup, or other disk," then select Continue and then "From another Mac or PC." The next window should show the Windows computer that you want to transfer files from. Click Continue, verify on the Windows computer that the passcodes match and click Continue again. Lastly, the assistant will ask you to select the types of files you want to transfer.

If you don't do the assistant right away, you can always use it later. There's no timeline for using it, so if you dig up an older Windows computer in the garage and want to transfer everything from it, the option will always be there.

Compatibility

Now that you have everything copied over, let's talk briefly about compatibility. While many files will open on a Mac, the software will not. That means if you have Word on Windows, you can't just move it over; most popular software (like Word) is available on the Mac, but you will have to purchase it.

Don't stress too much; most the files that you have just transferred will actually still open even if you don't buy software to open them. Word files (Doc, Docx) for example, will open in Pages (which is free on new Macs).

If your file does not open, then you will probably be able to find free software online that will open it.

Setup Assistant

If you are starting up the Mac for the first time (and you are the first owner), then the first thing that will happen is an automated setup assistant will guide you through creating an account and getting everything set up.

The first thing you'll do is select your country; if you don't see yours, then click See All. Click Continue after you finish each section. Next, you'll choose your keyboard layout; if you are an English speaker, then the United States is probably your first bet, but if you are going to be typing primarily in another language (like Chinese) then you may want to pick that country instead—this can be changed later.

Picking the wireless network is the next thing you will see after clicking Continue—you don't have to set up wireless at this point, but if you do, it will also trigger the Migration Assistant (which will help you transfer files); this is all optional so you can skip it (you can also come back to it later).

The next screen is one of the most important: entering your Apple ID. If you have any other Apple devices (iPad, iPod, iPhone, etc.) or if you have an ID that you use with Windows, then you'll want to use it because all of the apps, music and other media you've paid for are tied to your account. If you don't have one, you'll have the option of getting one—it's free and includes iCloud (also free), which I'll be talking about later.

The next part of the setup is Find My Mac (which you need iCloud for); this is a great feature that lets you see where your Mac is from your Internet browser; if it's been stolen it also lets you wipe away all of your content.

After agreeing to the terms, you'll be taken to the Time Zone selection. After that, you are asked if you want to enable the iCloud Keychain. What's the iCloud Keychain? Basically, this stores passwords in the Cloud so you can use them on any device.

Next, decide if you want to send diagnostics and usage data to Apple; this is all for statistical purposes to help Apple make their software and hardware better, but it's entirely up to you. It won't slow your computer down if you do decide to do it—it's all done in the background. After this step, you decide if you want to register your installation with Apple.

Finally, you are ready to start using your Mac!

[3] New To OS Big Sur

This chapter will cover:

- What's new in the latest update?

Big Sur OS is the latest operating system available for Macs. While Big Sur is free, it is not available to all devices; if you have an older Mac, then it may be time to upgrade to get all the best new features. The following devices are compatible, as of this writing:

- 2015 and later MacBook
- 2013 and later MacBook Air
- 2013 and later MacBook Pro
- 2014 and later Mac mini
- 2014 and later iMac
- 2017 and later iMac Pro

- 2013 and later Mac Pro

It should also be noted that not all features are available on older models. So if you hear someone talking about a great new feature on their Mac and you don't see it, then it's probably because you have an older Mac..

If you aren't sure what model number you have, go the Apple icon in the upper left corner of your screen, then click About This Mac.

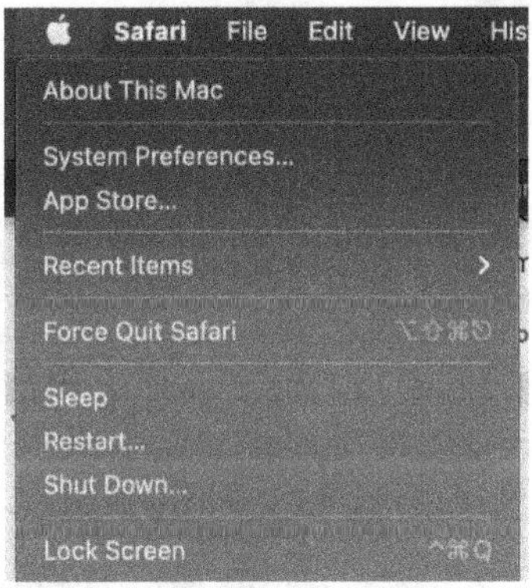

This will show you what OS you're running, the type of computer you have, and the serial number.

In terms of the overall look of Big Sur, there are two big changes: a Control Center that is reminiscent of what you see on iOS, and an enhanced messaging app. Both will be covered in greater scope later in this book. In terms of new features, the biggest ones you should be aware of are below:

- **Control Center** - A feature that has been on iPhone and iPads for years makes its way to macOS; control all of your settings in one easy to find place.
- **Safari** - Safari has been overhauled to make a much more personal experience; you can now have a customized start page, tab browsing is easier, and you can translate any page into another language.
- **Maps** - Maps gets a minor update with Big Sur; in addition to all the different types of directions that you can get (like walking, driving and transit), you can now get cycling directions. The app can also give you electric vehicle routing to help you find the best directions that include charging locations.
- **Redesigned Messages** - Message comes with several new features; the best: pinning conversations, so you can keep the people you talk to most up high; the reply to mention someone in a group reply, and reply directly to specific messages within a text exchange.

- **Password Monitoring** - Password monitoring alerts you when there's a data breach somewhere that you have a password stored, so you can change it right away and prevent identity theft.

That may not seem like a lot, but there are a lot more that are either minor or just aesthetic changes. For example, many apps have a cleaner look and refreshed sidebars; the dock has a more uniformed shape for app icons; and search is even faster. If you use AirPods with a Mac and iPhone / iPad / Apple Watch, switching between them is automatic. You no longer have to manually disconnect, then reconnect to the next device.

[3]

THE BASICS

This chapter will cover:

- Magic Mouse and ForceTouch
- The desktop
- Dark mode
- Dynamic mode
- Stacked icons
- Menu
- The Dock
- Split View
- Tabbed software
- Picture-in-picture video

The best way to learn is by doing, so I'm sure you're eager to get your hands wet and start using the Mac! If you are new to Mac, however, that can be a little intimating—it's not hard to use, but you have to, at the very least, know what you are looking at. In this chapter, I'll give you a crash course in the MacOS interface. By the end of the chapter, you won't be an expert, but you'll know where things are and how to start opening and using things.

KEYBOARD

The keyboard?! I know what you're thinking: a keyboard is a keyboard! Well, sort of. While it is true that you could use a Windows keyboard on a Mac, there are keyboards (including the one that's free with your Mac or built into your MacBook) that are specifically designed for Mac.

There are not a lot of differences; below are the four main ones.

Apple Key

On a Windows keyboard, there is a button that looks like a Windows flag called the Windows Button. There's no sense putting a Windows button on a Mac keyboard, so where the Windows button normally is, you'll find the Apple button, which doesn't look at all like an apple! It actually looks like this (⌘); it's more commonly known as the Command Button—though some people also call it the Clover Key and Pretzel Key.

Delete (Backspace)

On a Windows keyboard, the backspace button is a 'Backwards Delete' key and the delete button is a 'Forward Delete' key (removing the space immediately after the cursor). On a Mac keyboard, the backspace key is labeled 'Delete' and is in exactly the same location as the Windows backspace key. Most Mac keyboards don't have a Forward Delete key anymore, though larger ones do—it's called "Del->". If you don't see it, you still can use forward delete by hitting the FN button (button left corner of your keyboard) and Delete button.

Force Touch

If you have the latest MacBook Air then you will have a brand new feature called Force Touch; Force Touch is something you'll soon see on all iPhones, iPads and pretty much every new Apple device—it's actually already on the Apple Watch. So what is it? It measures how much pressure you are giving the Trackpad—if you tap down on your Trackpad over an icon or image, and then press all the way, it will show you a preview of it.

On iPhones this feature is called "3D Touch"; it's a little different, but it's basically the same.

You can change your Force Touch settings by going into System Preference and Mouse / Trackpad.

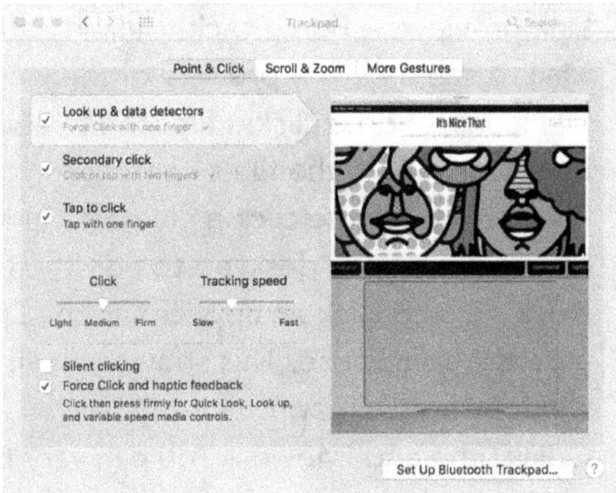

You'll notice when you push down on your Trackpad, it feels like it's clicking twice; when your computer is off, it won't feel like that because you need the computer powered on for the force feedback to work.

Here's a brief overview of some of the things you can do with Force Touch; as you use your Mac, you'll discover dozens and dozens more—especially as developers begin to implement it in software.

- Look up – Force click the text in a webpage and a popover appears, showing you Lookup results for that text. It may be a dictionary, Wikipedia page or something else.
- Addresses – Force click an address to see a Maps preview of that location.
- Events – Force click dates and events to add them to Calendar.

- Link previews – Force click a link in Safari or Mail to see an inline preview of the webpage.
- File icons – Force click a file icon to see a Quick Look preview of the file's content.
- File names – Force click a file name in the Finder or on your desktop to edit the file name.
- Dock – Force click an app icon in the Dock to access App Exposé. This shows you all open windows for that app.
- QuickTime and iMovie – You can vary the pressure you use on fast-forward and rewind buttons.
- Map zooming – Press harder on a zoom button to accelerate as you zoom in and out of a map.

THE DESKTOP

Hopefully, by now, your files are transferred, you've completed the initial startup, and you have a pretty picture on your desktop. At last, you are ready to use your computer!

The desktop is where you'll be spending much of your time, so let's take some time getting to know it.

The first thing you should notice is that it's really not that much different from Windows—it's a vast space that you can either leave empty or fill with icons or documents.

Apple Has a Dark Secret

Deep in the halls of Apple, developers have been working on something very...dark. It's called Dark Mode. Does anyone want to guess what happens when you switch it on? If you said "Disney emoji's dance happily on your screen" then go back and reread the question. So, what is dark mode and why would you want to use it?

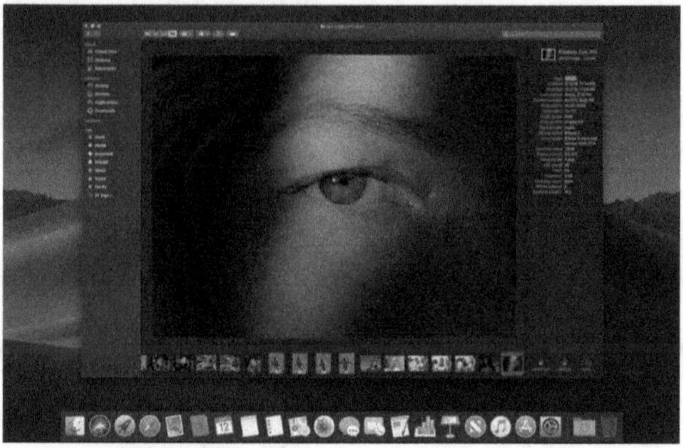

The point of dark mode is to put an emphasis on what you are working on or what you need to find. Let's say you're editing a photo. What's important? The photo. All those things in the background are just noise. Sometimes you need the noise for what you're working on, but you'll work more effectively by having them darkened. It's not like things in the background are harder to see—the contrast just helps you be more creative. At least that's what Apple thinks. If you think otherwise, you have the option to turn it off.

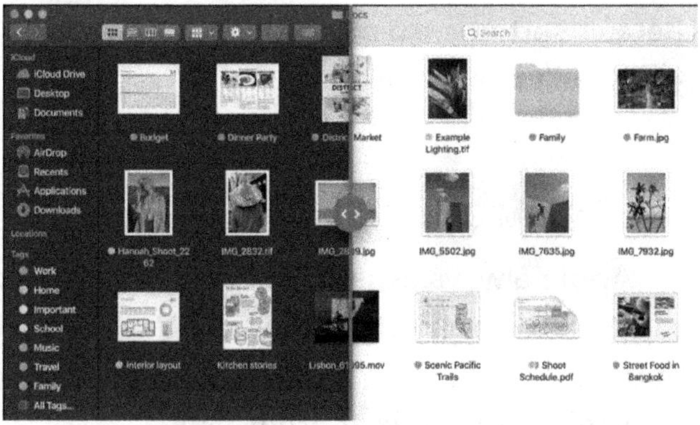

In the image above, you can see the difference between dark mode (left) and light mode (right). In dark mode, those thumbnails should pop a little more than in light mode.

Not all apps will look different. It's up to the company that makes the app to redesign an app that takes advantage of it. Apple has obviously updated many of its apps (like Calendar, iTunes, Mail).

If you've updated to MacOS Catalina then you'll be asked if you want it on. If you want to turn it on, or if you turned it off but now want it on, it's easy to do:

Go to System Preferences (you'll find that in the app launch area of your Dock).

Select General and select the option.

When you're in System Preferences > General, you'll also notice you have the option to change the accent color that goes along with light / dark mode; this changes all the arrows, toggles, etc. throughout the OS. You can always go back to default settings, so don't be afraid to play around: you won't break anything!

IT'S DYNAMIC!

Apple always likes to put emphasis on making things more aesthetically pleasing when they update the OS. Dark mode is one way they do that; Dynamic Desktop is another.

When I heard the name, I imagined it would let your wallpaper come alive by having something more...dynamic—like the wallpaper could be a looped video or something. It's a little less dynamic than that, unfortunately, but still a cool feature.

So what is it? Well, the wallpaper on your desktop will change, but it's a little slower. Basically, the wallpaper changes appearance depending on what time of day it is. So in Apple's example, there's an image of the Mojave desert; in the morning it's bright and throughout the day it gets darker.

To use it, make sure you have Location Series on—the OS has to know what time it is in your time zone.

THIS OS IS STACKED

Mac excels in many ways; one of the biggest ways is in how it keeps you organized. Apple is always working hard thinking about how to help you stay organized and keep all your content structured in a way that makes it easy to find.

Apple is a bit like a library; other OSes are a bit like used bookstores. Both places have the same thing: books. But one is organized in a way to help you find what you need quickly; the other is organized in a way where you really need to browse for things.

If your desktop looks a little like the below image, then Stacks can help.

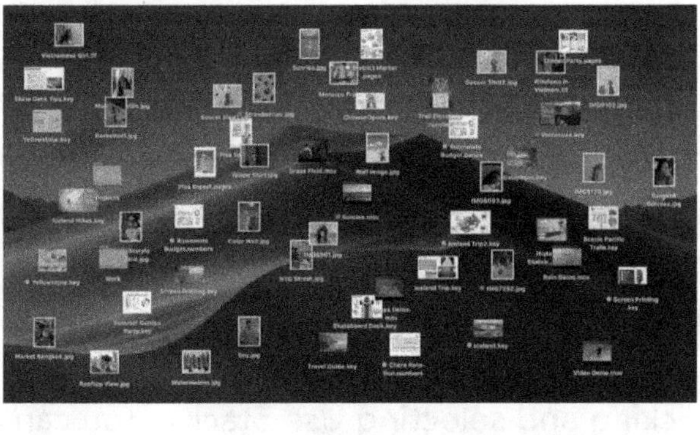

How does Stacks clean this mess up? When it's enabled, the above screenshot would look a bit like the below one.

Everything is still there, but it's grouped together. All the images, documents, and movies are in one group. If you want to see anything within that group, then just click the thumbnail and it will expand. If you add a new file to your desktop, it's automatically put in the appropriate group.

If you're on your desktop, you can turn it on by clicking and selecting Use Stacks. You can also do this by going into Finder and then choosing Use Stacks. You can also pick how you want things stacked. By default, it's by kind, but you can also stack by date or tag.

If you want to turn it off, repeat the process above but uncheck Use Stacks.

Menu Bar

One of the most noticeable differences between Windows and Mac on the desktop is the top menu bar. I'll be referring back to this menu bar throughout the book, but right now what you need to know is this bar changes with each program that you open, but some of the features remain the same. The little apple, for instances, never changes—clicking on this will always bring up options to restart, shut down, or log out of your computer. The little magnifying glass at the far right is also always there. Any time you click on that, you can search for files, emails, contacts, etc., that are on your computer.

Menulets

At the top right, you'll see several "menulets," which include Bluetooth, wireless connectivity, volume, battery, time and date, the name of the account currently logged in, Spotlight, and

Notifications, as well as other assorted third-party icons (if installed).

As this book continues, we'll refer back to this part of the menu.

Control Center

If you have other Apple devices, then you might notice that things on the Mac look a little familiar. That's on purpose. Each update, Macs add new features that resemble what you find on iPhones and iPads. It helps make the experience more friction-free, which makes it easier to get things up and running.

This is especially true with the Control Center, which is on the top menu right next to the Siri icon. Clicking on it will bring up a series of options. This is where you can change the Wi-Fi, mirror your screen, and more.

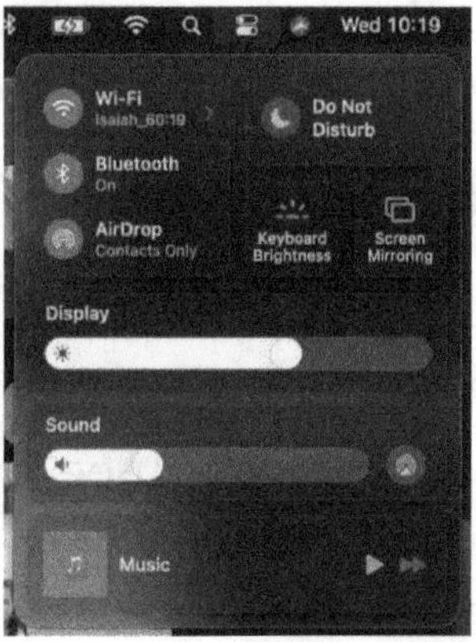

It may not look like a lot of options, but each control has subcontrols. Just click on the arrow next to it.

Dock

Windows has a taskbar on the bottom of the screen, and Mac has a Dock; the Dock is where all your commonly used applications are.

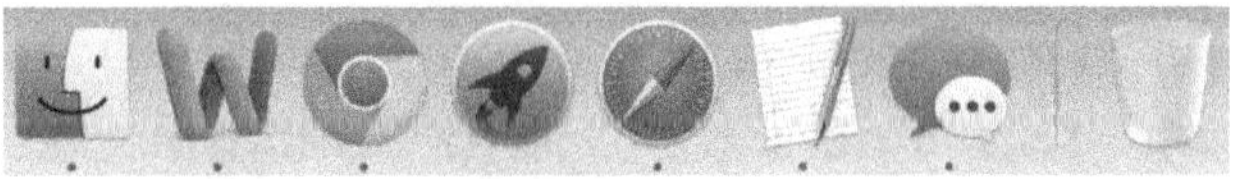

If you see a little dot under the icon, then the program is currently open. If you want to close it, then click the icon with two fingers to bring up the options, and then click Quit.

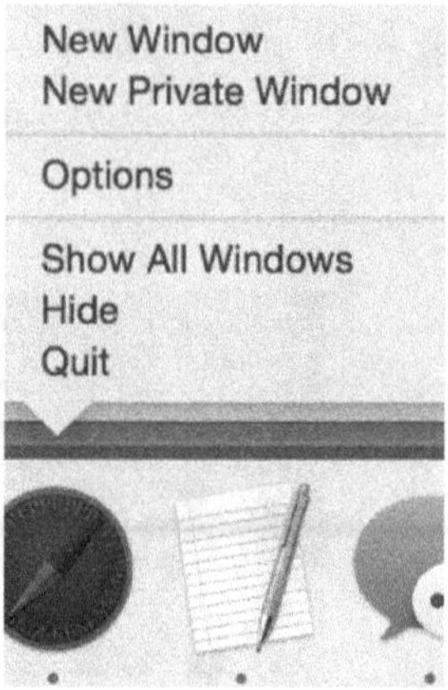

Removing a program from the Dock is pretty simple—just drag the icon to the Trash and let go. This will not remove the program—it only removes the shortcut. Finder, Trash, and Launchpad are the only programs that you cannot remove.

If you want to add a program to the Dock, then open it; when the icon appears on the Dock, click with two fingers, then go to Options and select Keep in Dock.

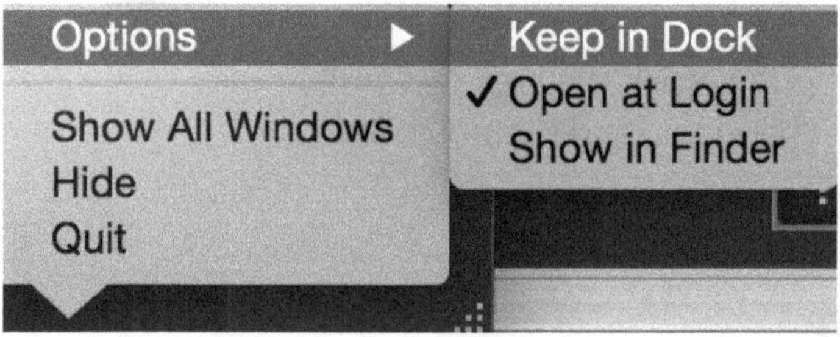

TRASH

At the right end of the Dock is the Trash. To delete a folder, file or application, drag the item to the Trash, or right-click (two-finger click) the item and select Move to Trash from the pop-up menu. If you want to eject a disk or drive, such as an iPod or USB flash drive, drag the volume into the Trash. As the volume hovers over the Trash, the icon morphs from a trash can to a large eject button. Release the mouse, and your volume will be safely ejected and can be removed from the computer. To empty the Trash, right-click (click with two fingers) on the Trash icon in the Dock, and select Empty Trash.

You can manage the Trash yourself, but I also highly recommend an app called "Clean My Mac" (https://macpaw.com/cleanmymac); it's a little expensive, but when I use it, it normally helps me free up 1GB of storage just by deleting installation files and extensions that I don't need.

APP BUTTONS

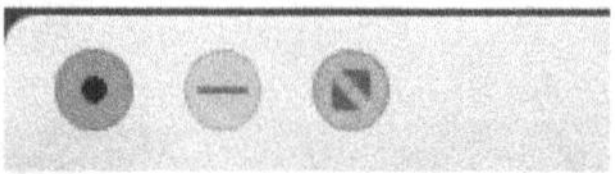

The little lights in the image above have no name. Some people call them traffic lights. You'll start seeing a lot of them because nearly all Mac programs use them. On a Windows, you've seen them as an X and a minus in the upper right of your screen. On a Mac, they appear in the upper left of the running program. The red light means close, the yellow light means minimize, and the green makes the app full screen.

Full screen means the program takes up the entire screen and even the Dock disappears. You can see the Dock and other programs quickly by swiping the Trackpad to the right with four fingers. To get back to the app, swipe with four fingers to your left.

LAUNCHPAD

Launchpad is essentially the Start menu on a Windows computer. It shows your programs.

When you click it, you'll see rows of programs; you can immediately start typing to search for an app, or you can just look for it. If you have a lot of apps, then you probably have more than one screen. Swipe with two fingers to the left to see the next screen.

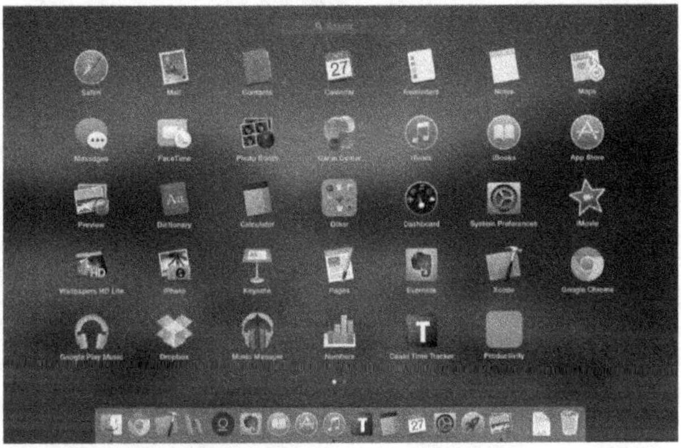

Launchpad takes a lot of cues from iPhone and iPad. If you want to remove a program, for example, you do it the same way you remove an iPhone or iPad app. Just click and hold until an X appears above it, then click the X to remove it. Similarly, to rearrange icons, use the same method for rearranging iPhone / iPad apps—click and hold over the icon until it begins to shake, and then move it wherever you want it to go. You can even put programs into groups the same way as an iPhone / iPad—click and hold over the icon, then drag it on top of the app you want to group it with; finally, when the folder appears, you can let go.

After you delete a program, you can re-download it anytime, by going into the App Store (as long as you downloaded it from the App Store and not from a website).

NOTIFICATIONS

For the past few updates, Apple has attempted to replicate iOS (iPad / iPhone) features; the move is meant to make using a Mac much like using a mobile device. This attempt at replicating features is especially true with Catalina OS.

Notification was a new feature to OS X Yosemite. You can find it on the top menu button at all times; it's to the far right-hand corner and looks like this:

Click it any time you want to see alerts. You can also access it by swiping with two fingers to the left from the edge of your Trackpad.

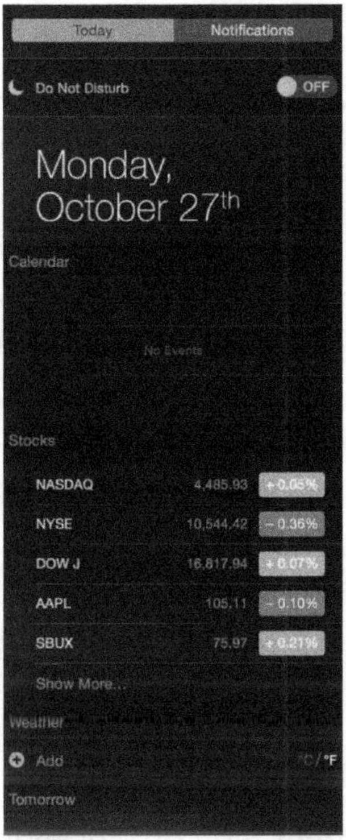

When you swipe down from the top of an iPad or iPhone you will get a similar screen. There are two parts of the Notifications menu: Today and Notifications.

The Today tab is where you'll see things happening more in the moment—what's the weather, what's in your calendar, what's going on with your stocks, etc. The Notifications tab is where you'll see things like Facebook messages or emails. Later in this book, I'll show you how to customize it.

Split View

Split view is perhaps the biggest added feature to OS X. It lets you run two apps side-by-side—but there's a catch: not all apps are compatible. So if you're scratching your head because this feature won't work for you, then chances are it's not that you are doing it wrong—it's that the app doesn't support the feature.

There are two ways to get the split view to work. Let's look at both of them. First, make sure the two apps that you want to run side-by-side are not running in full screen mode.

Method 1

Click and hold the green button in the upper left corner of your app.

A transparent blue box will appear; drag and drop the app into it (by default, the blue is on the left side, but if you drag to the right side, it will also turn blue and you can drop it in).

Next, click the program you want to use side-by-side.

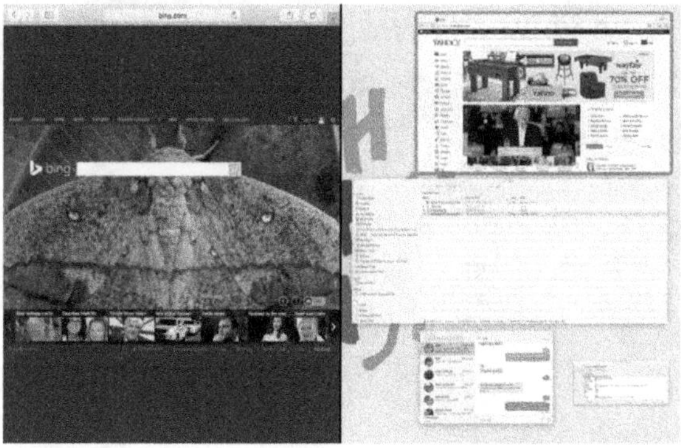

A side-by-side window now appears; you can use the middle black line to make one bigger or smaller, by dragging left or right.

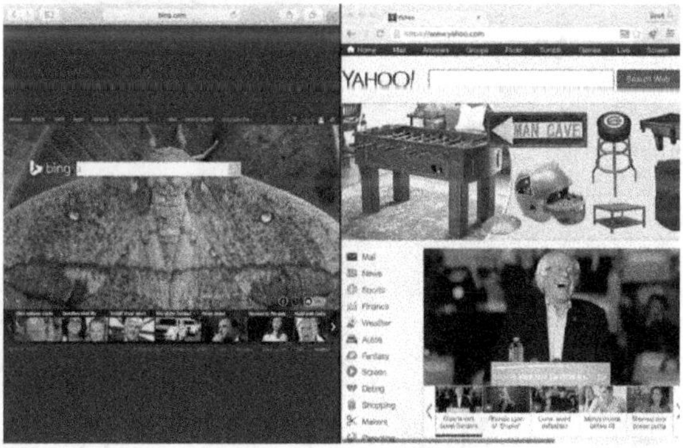

To return to the normal view, click the green button in the upper left corner of the app once more (you can also hit the ESC key on your keyboard).

Method 2

As you are probably noticing, most things in OS X can happen by several different methods; side-by-side view has two. The second way to get apps is to open your Mission Control, and drag the app to the top menu.

You'll notice, a grey box appears and the box appears to split.

Once you drop the app into that box, you'll see a side-by-side preview. Once you click the preview, it will maximize.

Returning to the non-split screen is done the same way as Method 1 (click the green box in the upper left corner or hit the ESC key on the keyboard).

Tabbed Software

If you've ever used Tabs on Internet Explorer or Chrome, then this next feature might interest you. It allows you to open documents (such as Maps and Pages) with tab viewing. Note: not all Mac apps support this feature.

To use it, open two windows of the same app. I'll use Maps in the example below.

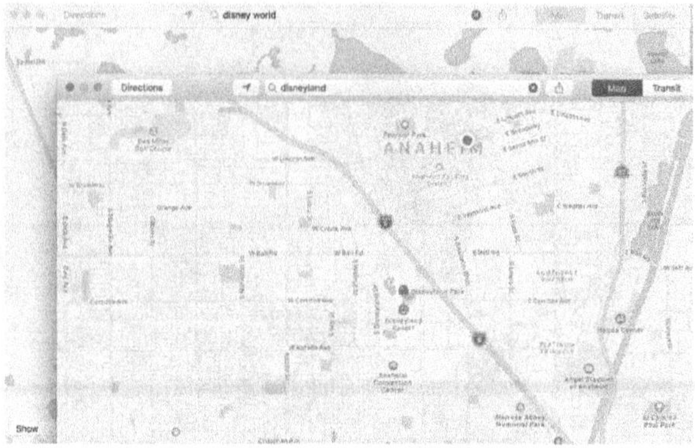

Next, go to Window and Merge All Windows.

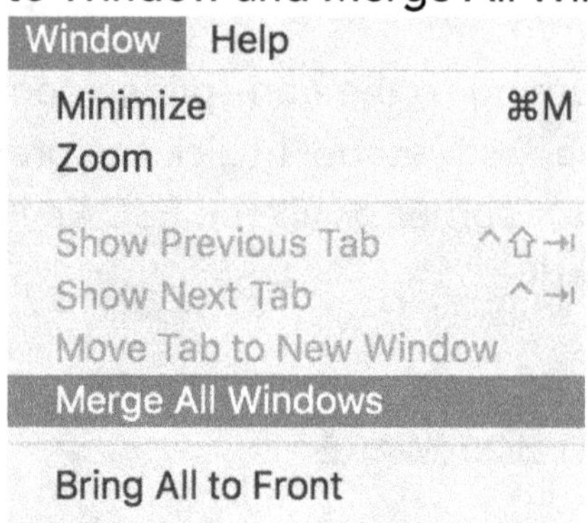

Your windows should now be merged.

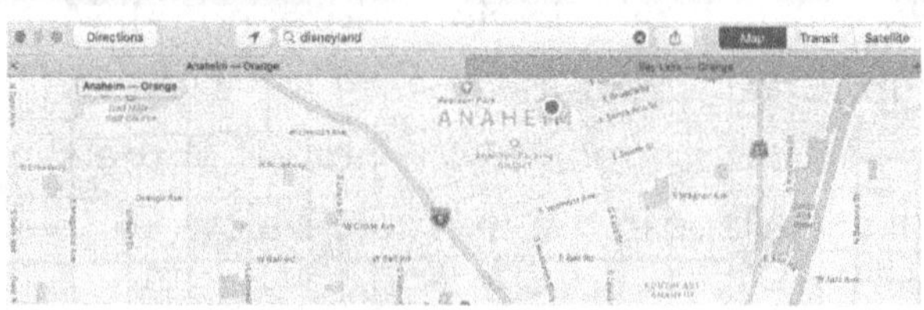

PICTURE-IN-PICTURE VIDEO

If you'd like to watch a video while you work, then you're in luck! If you already own the video (a video you purchased on iTunes, for example), then just start playing the video and go to View and Float on Top.

But what about Web videos? Such as Vimeo and YouTube? That's easy too. Just double-click the video you are watching, and select Enter Picture-In-Picture.

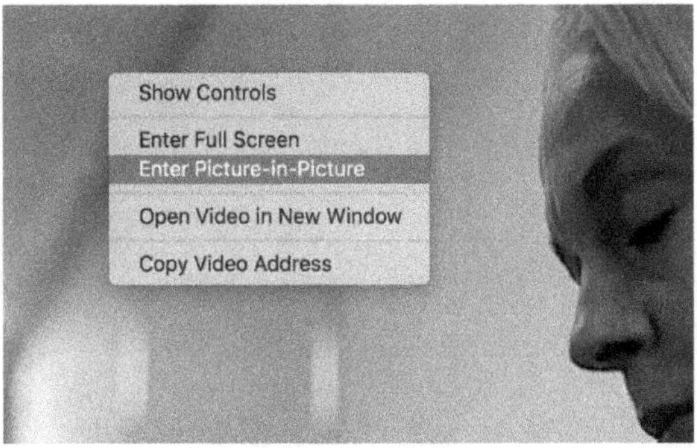

Your video will immediately begin playing above other windows.

[4]

WHERE IS EVERYTHING?

This chapter will cover:

- Finder
- Gallery view
- Other views in Finder
- Finder tabs
- Tags

One of the greatest things about Mac is how easy it is to find things. Sure, Windows has a search, but it feels clunky and doesn't always work the way you expect. I'll cover how to find things in this chapter.

Finder

The first icon on your Dock—one of three that cannot be deleted or moved—is the Finder icon.

Finder is the Mac equivalent of Explorer on a Windows computer; as the name implies, it finds things. Finder is pretty resourceful and powerful so this section will be a little longer than others because there's a lot you can do with it.

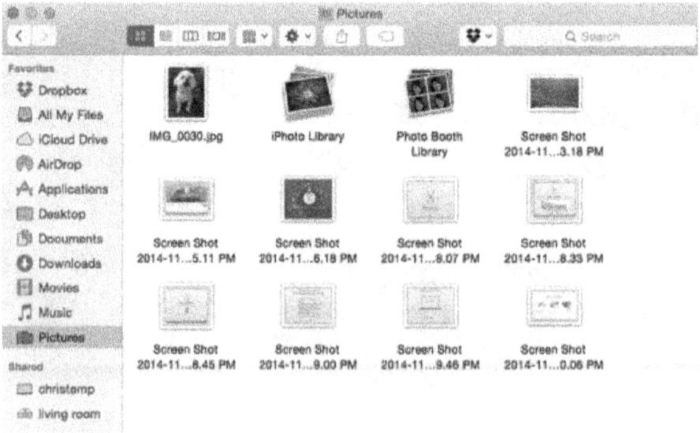

Let's get started by clicking on the Finder icon.

Finder Reimagined

Finder is how you find things on a Mac—clever name, right? Like a lot of things in MacOS, there are similarities between how it works on Mac and iPhone. Mojave added a few new features still present in Catalina you should know about, however.

Gallery View

There are several different types of views in Finder (where you find things—like File Explorer in Windows). Examples of views are: list, columns, and icons. Gallery view was a new view in Mojave that you still see in Catalina.

Gallery view displays a large preview of the file with thumbnails of everything else in the directory below it. And by "preview" this isn't just for images where you can see what the image looks like—this works across all kinds of docs. If it's a PDF, for example, you can see a preview of the PDF.

To the right of the file, there's a side panel that will tell you the more detailed metadata for the file.

Quick Actions

Apple is all about efficiency; to be more efficient, it helps to be able to do things a little quicker. That's where Quick Actions help. With Quick Actions, you can, for example, change the orientation of a file or add password protection. The actions available depend on the type of file.

OTHER VIEWS

There are four other ways to view folders on your Mac—icons, lists, columns, and Cover Flow. Different views make sense for different file types, and you can change the view using the View Options icons (pictured below).

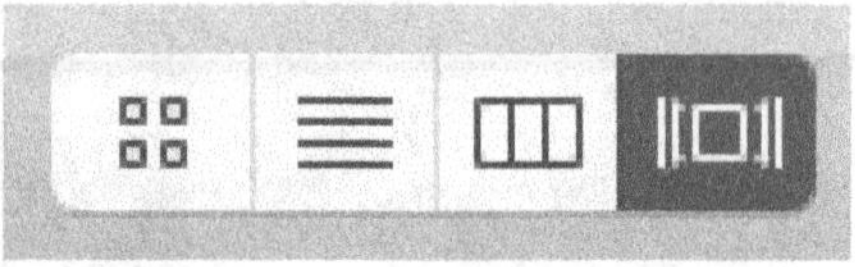

Cover Flow View

Cover Flow lets you quickly go through thumbnails / previews of photos (it's a little like Film Strip in Windows); you can also sort any of the columns by clicking on the header—so if you are looking for a larger file, then click the Size column, or if you are looking for a recent file, then pick the Date Modified column.

Icon View

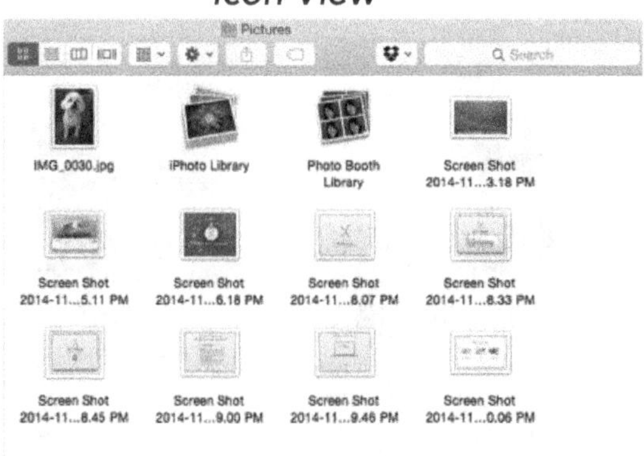

Icon View can help if you need to sort through several image files or applications. It gives you either a thumbnail of each picture or an icon for each file or app.

List View

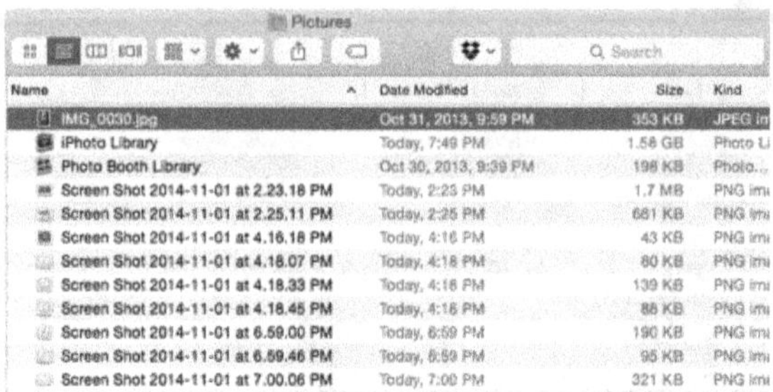

List View, on the other hand, gives you more information about the file, including the date it was last modified. This is the perfect view for sorting.

Column View

Finally, Column View which is kind of a hybrid of List View and Cover Flow View. It shows the folder hierarchy a file is located in. Notice that Finder doesn't include the Windows "go up one level" button—Column View is a good way to get the same results and navigate easily through your file structure.

SORTING IN FINDER

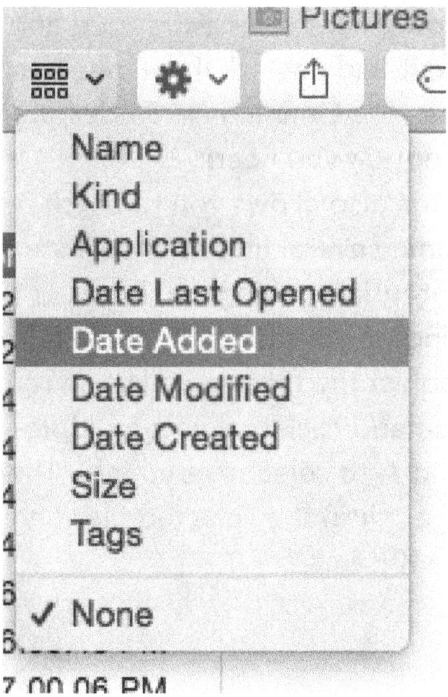

Finder gives you a number of ways to sort your files and folders. You can sort by name, type, the application required for opening the file (like

Microsoft Word, for example), the date the file was created, modified, or opened, the file size, and any tags you may have applied.

File Management

Most file management tasks in OS X are similar to Windows. Files can be dragged and dropped, copied, cut and pasted. If you need to create a new folder, use the Gear icon in Finder, which will give you the option you need.

Catalina also allows you to batch rename files (i.e. rename several files at once instead of one at a time), potentially saving you hours of time, depending on your file system. To take advantage of this, select the files you'd like to rename (hint: use Command-click to select multiple files, or use Command-A to select everything). Then right-click (two-finger click) the selected files and choose "Rename X Items."

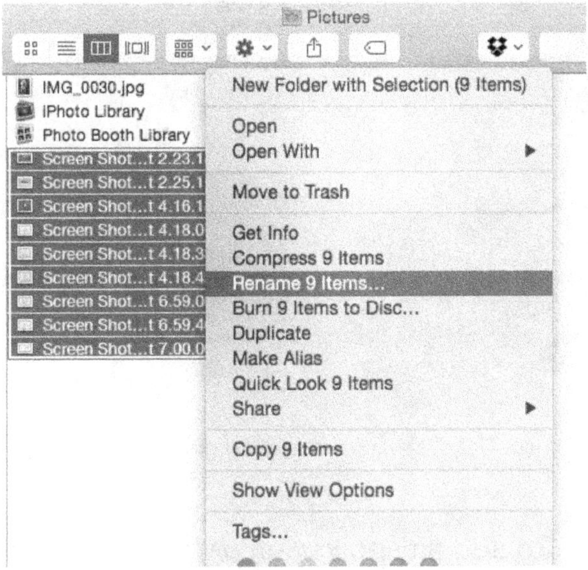

You'll then have the option to replace text or to add text to the file names.

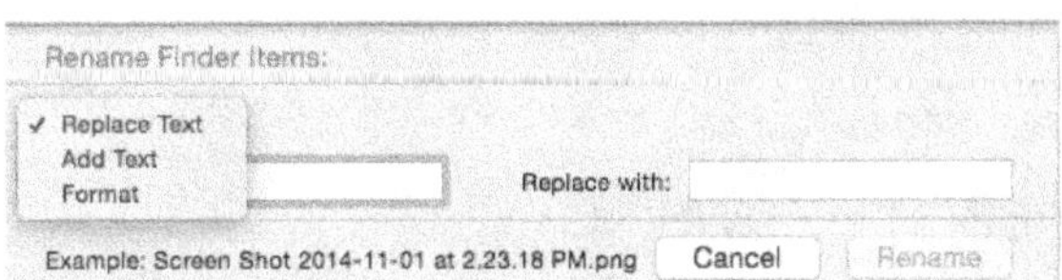

Favorites

If you look on the left side of the Finder Window, you'll see a Favorites sidebar. This section includes high-frequency folders, like Documents, Pictures, Downloads, and more.

To add an application or file to your Favorites menu, just drag it over to the Favorites area and drop it. To remove an item from Favorites, right-click it (click with two fingers) and select Remove From Sidebar.

Tabbed Browsing

Apple took a page from Internet browsers by adding something called "Tabbed Browsing" to Finder. Basically, instead of having several Finder boxes open (which is how you had to do it in older OSes) you open tabs. To open an additional Finder tab, press Command-T or click File and New Tab.

If you want to merge all of your tabbed windows, just click Windows in the file menu on the top of your screen, and then Merge All Windows.

TAGS

If you use photo apps like Flickr, then you probably know all about tagging; it's essentially adding subjects to your file to make it easier to find. Let's say the file is regarding the 2015 tax year—you can add a tag to the file called "2015 Taxes" or whatever you want it to be. You can also color code it.

To assign a tag to a file (you can also assign it to a folder), click the file / folder with two fingers, and then click tags; if this is your first tag just type it in and hit Enter; if you've already tagged a file and want to use the same name, then click the name of the tag as it appears.

[5]

How Do I Do All the Things I Want to Do?

This chapter will cover:

- Setting up Internet
- Browsing with Safari
- Setting up and sending email

The Mac is a beautiful machine, but you can only admire that desktop for so long; eventually, you'll want to get on the Internet—how else will you get your daily dose of cat memes or keep in touch with the Nigerian prince trying to give you money? I'll show you how in this chapter.

There are two methods: Ethernet (i.e. plugging in a LAN cable to your computer) and Wireless.

Setting Up With Ethernet

All new Mac computers are set up with Wi-Fi; iMacs also have Ethernet ports to plug in a network cable. This option isn't available on any of the Mac laptops—though you can buy an adapter if you absolutely must have it.

If you have a basic Internet modem, then set up is pretty easy. Just plug a network cable into your Internet hub, and plug the other end into your Mac. Once it's plugged in, the Internet should work.

Newer Macs come with top of the line wireless radios for Wi-Fi, so you should be perfectly fine without using the Ethernet port.

Setting Up Wireless Networks

Setting up a wireless connection is also pretty simple. Just click the Wi-Fi menu on the menu bar. It looks like the image below and is near the upper right corner:

As long as there's a wireless network in range, it will show up when you click it (sometimes it does take a few seconds to appear).

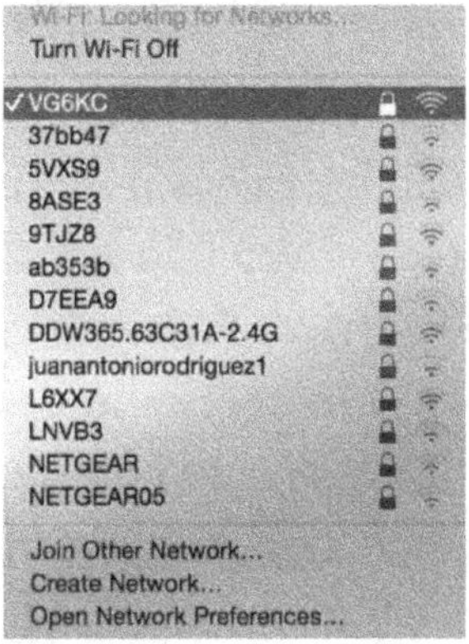

If there's a lock next to the Wi-Fi name, then you'll need to know the passcode (if it's a home Internet connection, then it's usually on the bottom of your Internet modem; if it's at a business, then you'll have to ask for the code. If there's no lock, then it's an open network. You usually see this kind of network at places like Starbucks.

If it's a locked network, then as soon as you click on it, it will ask for the code; once it's entered and you click Connect, then you're connected (assuming you added it right); if it's not locked then once you click on it, it will attempt to connect.

AIRPORT EXPRESS / AIRPORT EXTREME

If you need more range in your wireless connection or want to set up a private network, Apple sells two Mac accessories. One is the Airport Express ($99) and the other is the Airport Extreme

($199, or $299 to $399 if you'd like the one with a hard drive).

The Express is a good option for people wanting to add a private network (so, for instance, you can have a network just for guest and guest printing); the Airport Extreme gives excellent range; I use one in my home because the modem supplied with my phone company could barely reach the next room over and the signal strength was weak; the Extreme not only got to the next room, but it got several more rooms—I can now get a signal more than 100 feet from where the Extreme is located. It's a pretty easy installation, and Apple has videos for those who need extra help.

The more expensive models are also a good option for backing up computers. The $299 and $399 models offer up to 3TB of storage; the way it works is your computer connects to it, and will back up your computer in the background, so your computer is always being backed up. These models also let you share files. So, for instance, if you want a private storage locker for anyone who connects to your network, then you could do so here.

SAFARI

(For an expanded overview of how to use Safari, see the bonus book at the end of this book)

Just as a Windows computer has Internet Explorer as the default web browser, Mac has Safari as the default web browser; if you've used Safari on your iPhone or iPad then you should already be accustomed to it.

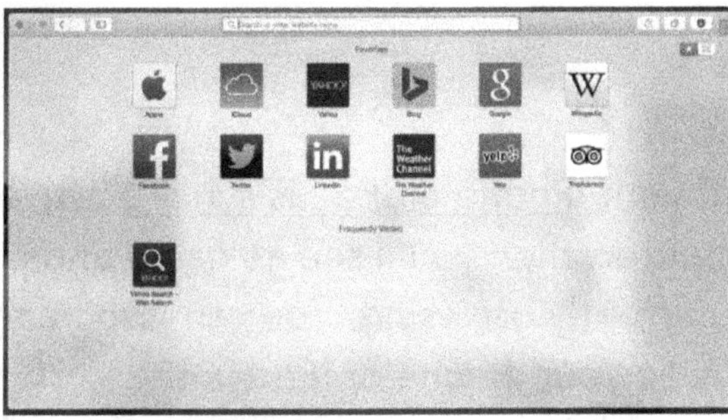

Noticeably absent from Safari is something called "Flash". Flash is what you might have used to watch some videos and other web apps; you can always download it, but this will affect the battery life of your laptop, as Flash tends to drain the battery quickly—which is one of the reasons Apple does not include it.

You are also free to download other Internet browsers. Some of the popular free ones are Google Chrome (www.google.com/chrome/), Mozilla Firefox (www.mozilla.org/firefox), and Opera (www.opera.com).

One of the biggest advantages of using Safari over another web browser is a feature called Handoff. Let's say you're reading an article on your phone on the subway coming into work; you get to work and want to pick up where you left off on a larger Mac screen; just open up Safari, then click the two square boxes in the upper right corner.

If your iPhone or iPad is synced with the computer, then you'll see its name and pages that it's currently browsing. You can also handoff a Mac page to your iPhone or iPad in the same way.

In addition to websites, handoff also lets you seamlessly sync things like maps, messages, and documents (Pages, Numbers, and Presentation documents).

Mail

Mail is the Mac equivalent of Outlook; like Safari, it works in a very similar way to iPad and iPhone. Apple will provide you with a free email address that ends @icloud.com, but you can also add normal email into the application (like Hotmail, Yahoo, and Gmail).

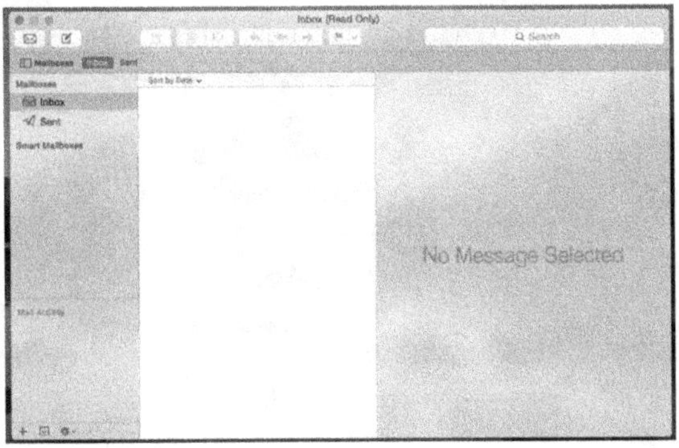

ADDING ACCOUNTS

To get started, you need to add your email account. Locate the Mail app by clicking on Launchpad, and then clicking the Mail app icon.

Once the app opens, go to the top menu bar and click Mail > Add Account. This will load the Add Account dialogue box.

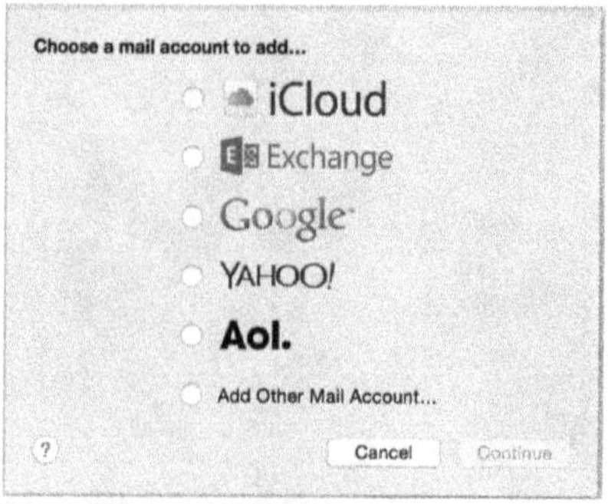

Select the provider that you will be adding in (Note: you can go back and add as many accounts as you want) and click Continue. Next, you'll be asked what your Name, Email Address, and Password are.

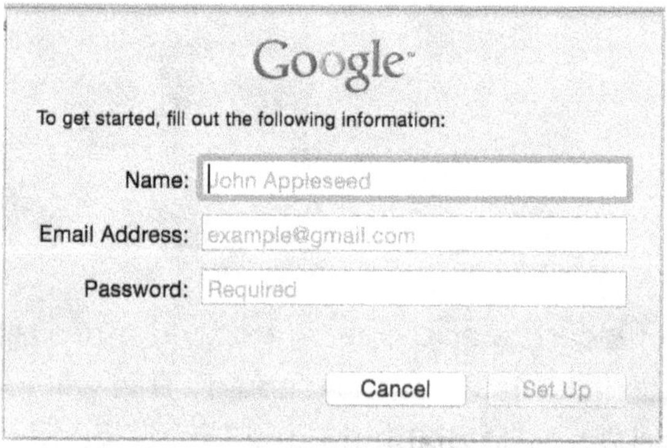

If you are using a popular email provider, set up is pretty self-explanatory. If you are using a business email, then you will probably need to work with your system administrator to get it added in correctly.

Once it's set up, you should start seeing mail show up on your computer.

SENDING AN EMAIL

Now that you have an account added, you can start sending mail; to send mail you can either press Command-N on your keyboard, go to the top menu and select File and New Message, or click the Compose icon (it looks like a pencil going through a square).

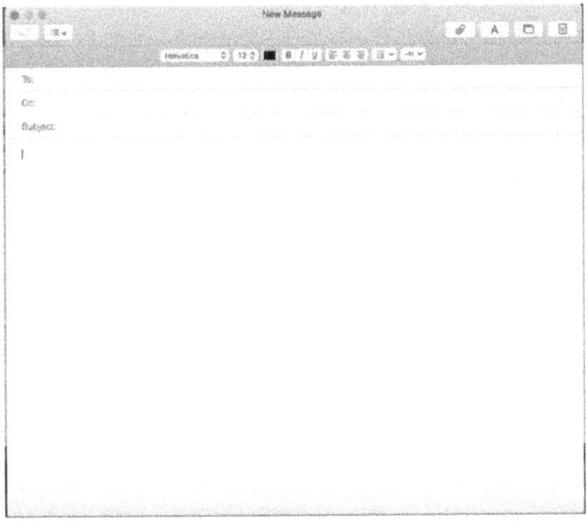

The New Message dialogue box will appear. In the To field, enter the email address or addresses that you'd like to send a message to, add in a subject and message, and then hit the paper airplane in the upper left corner when you are ready to send the message.

You can also add formatting to the message by clicking on the "A" button. Formatting is very basic—you can bold, add italics, underline, and change the coloring.

[6]

THERE'S AN APP FOR THAT

This chapter will cover:

- Phone calls
- Contacts
- Message
- FaceTime
- Photo Booth
- Calendar
- Reminders
- Notes
- iTunes
- App Store
- Siri
- Mac meets iOS

Now that you know about how Mac works (and how to find cat memes), I'm going to talk about the pre-installed programs.

Phone Calls

Apple products really work best with other Apple products; that's even truer with Catalina, where you can sync your iPhone account to make phone calls (both video and regular) and send messages right from your Mac. Additionally, you can even use your iPhone's data connection to get the Internet on your laptop on the go—this is especially handy while travelling if you don't want to pay for Wi-Fi spots that charge for access (just keep in mind that your data connection does have monthly limits and using a computer can go through those limits very quickly—in other words, this probably isn't something you want to do to stream Netflix movies).

CONTACTS

Unless you are a business person, having contacts on your computer might not seem necessary; here's the advantage of it—it syncs with your phone. So having a contact on your computer will carry over to your other mobile devices. To use it, go to your Launchpad, then click the icon.

If you're signed into iCloud, then you should see dozens of contacts already. To create a new contact, click on the (+) button at the bottom of the main window. On the next screen add all the info you want—it can be as much or as little as you desire. Some contacts may only need a website address, others might have mailing address—it's entirely up to you how much information you add. You can also edit a contact by finding their name, then clicking on the Edit button. If you want to delete someone, then find their name and hit Delete on your keyboard (you can also delete by clicking on their name with two fingers).

Message

When you use Messages from your Mac to send messages just keep in mind that it's kind of like instant messaging for Mac users—that means it's designed to work with Mac products...nothing else.

Setting Up Message

1. To set up Message, click the Messages icon to launch it.
2. If you were already logged into iCloud on the Mac, you will automatically be logged into Message.
3. If you'd like to change this account or haven't yet logged in, select Messages > Preferences on the top menu bar.

4. When the Accounts dialogue box comes up, click on the Accounts tab.
5. In the left-hand window, you will see Message. Select it.
6. The following screen will prompt you to enter the email address and password associated with iCloud. Do so and click the blue Sign In button to complete the setup process.

Setting Up Other IM Clients

While Message is made for Mac products, you can use it for other messaging services like Google, Yahoo, and AOL.

To add other instant messaging (IM) clients to Messages:

1. Open up Messages if it isn't already running.
2. On the top menu bar, click Messages > Add Account.

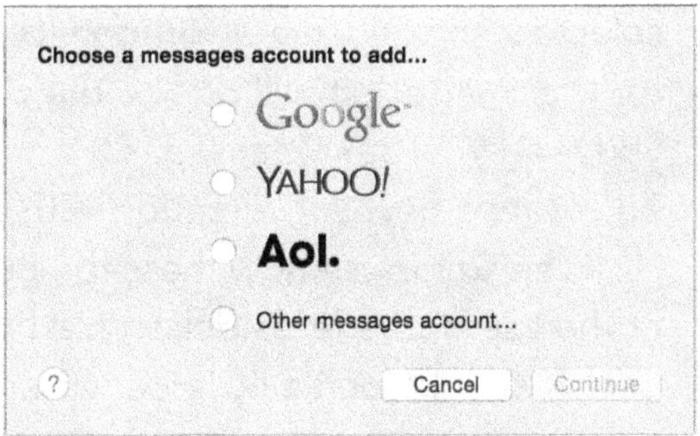

3. Select the type of account that you'd like to add, such as Gmail or Yahoo, and select Continue.
4. You will be prompted to enter the appropriate email address and password, and click the Set Up button to finish.

So now that it's set up, how do you send a message?

Start New Conversation

1. Before we begin, take a look at the entire Messages screen. It should be totally empty with no conversations. On the left sidebar it will say No Conversations. This is where you will be able to change between different conversations with people by clicking on each one. On the right-hand side, you will also see No Conversation Selected. Here is where you will be able to type new messages and read everything in whatever conversation is currently selected. If you have an iPhone (or any phone for that matter), it will be like the screen where you read your text messages.
2. To create a new conversation with someone, click the Compose new message button located at the top of the left sidebar, next to the search bar. It should look a little pencil inside of a square.

When you get a message, if your sound is enabled, you'll get a little chime.

Tapbacks

If you've used Stickers on the iPad and iPhone, you might be disappointed to see that feature has not yet arrived on MacOS. There is one feature from iOS: Tapbacks. Tapbacks let you respond to a message to indicate you like what the message says or that you agree with it. To use it, right-click (two-finger click) on any message and select your response.

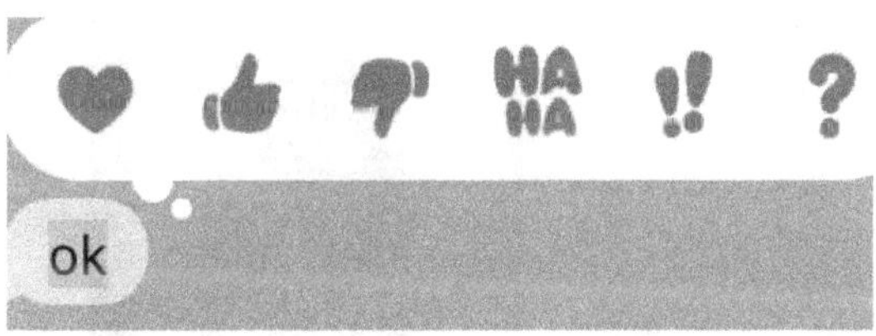

Pinning Messages

If you text a lot, then it might get a little cumbersome replying. The way Messages works is the most recent conversations go to the top. This mostly works well, but you can also pin favorites to the top.

In the example below, my wife is pinned to the top of the conversations. Even though other people have written to me more recently, she will always be up there (unless I remove her). That makes it easy to reply.

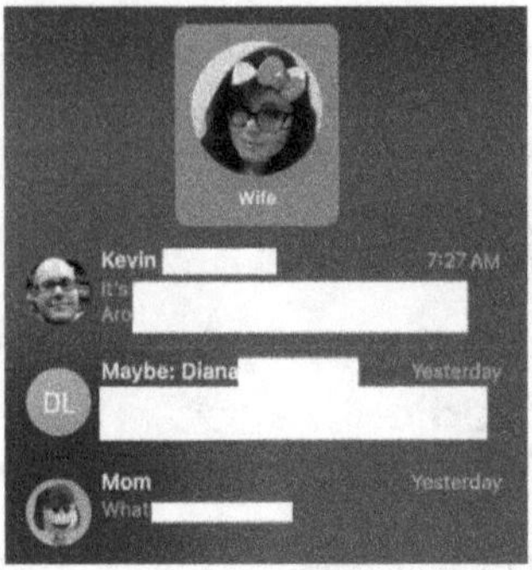

To add or remove someone from the top, drag / swipe with your mouse over the message, then tap the pin.

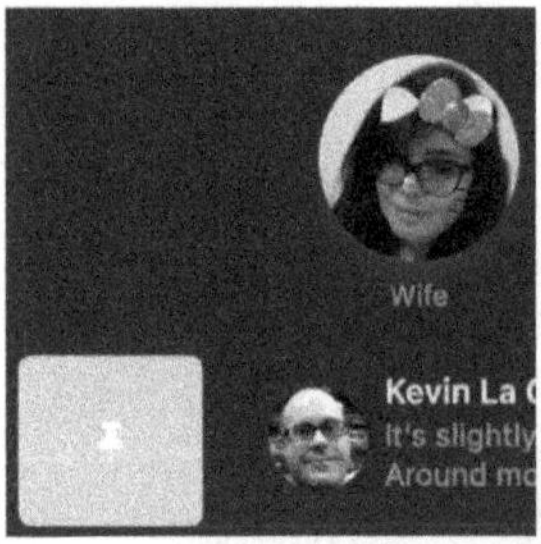

If you want to remove them, right click the message, and select unpin.

You can have several people pinned to the top. Personally, I find three is good, but you can add even more.

Message Tagging

If you have used messaging programs like Slack, then you are probably all too familiar with tagging someone in a conversation. Tagging gets the person's attention and starts a new thread within the conversation.

So if you are in a large text message exchange, then when you tag someone, everyone can read it, but everyone is not notified. So it's a little less obtrusive.

To tag someone in a conversation, just put an @ in front of their name when you reply.

Replying to Messages

Obviously, you can reply to a message by typing the message in the box and pressing return on your keyboard. But that only replies to the last message. What if the message is several threads up? Or what if it's a group and you want to reply to one particular message from a specific person?

To reply to a message that's higher up, right click over that message, and then select reply.

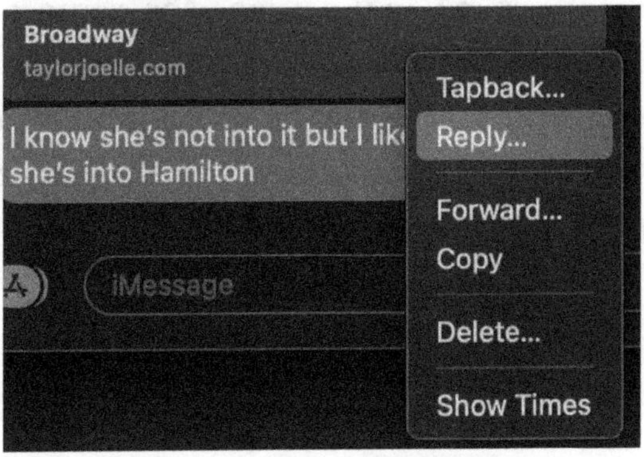

When you do this, the message will show up with a reply underneath it.

It will also show up as the last message sent but with an arrow notifying the user that you've replied to something in particular.

FaceTime

FaceTime allows you to connect with friends and family using your computer's built-in camera. I've heard people say they are so worried that someone is watching them through their webcam that they cover it with tape. When FaceTime is in use (i.e. when the camera is on and people can see you) a bright green light comes on—so you don't have to worry about people spying on you…if you don't see the light, then the camera is off.

The app can be launched by clicking on Launchpad > FaceTime.

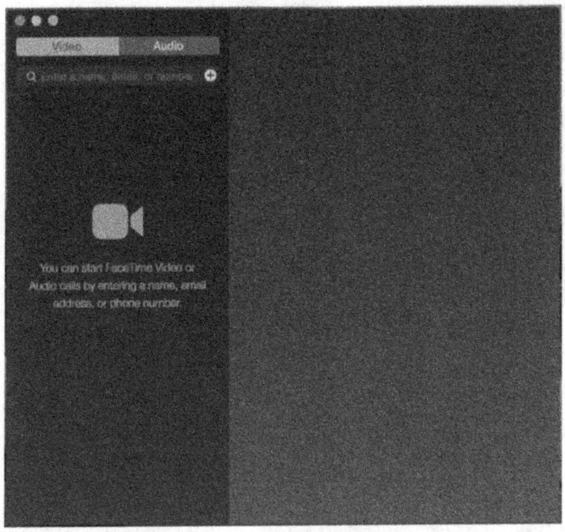

On the left side you can enter a person's name if they are in your Contacts, or a phone number. For FaceTime to work, the other person must also have an Apple device, and accept your call.

You can also use FaceTime audio. This lets you call someone without the camera—it's essentially a Wi-Fi phone call.

Photo Booth

We're a culture of selfies, so it's appropriate to talk about the app that takes your picture.

To get started, go to Launchpad and click the Photo Booth icon.

Couple of things you should notice once the app loads. First, you! If you look to the top of your screen, there should be a green light. That tells you the camera is on. But now click on a different app in your Dock—see how the green light goes off? And now click on the Photo Booth icon again, and once again the green light is on. What's going on with that light? The light indicates your camera is on—but it only stays on while you are in the Photo Booth app.

Are you ready to take a picture? Put on your silly face and click the camera button.

Like a lot of Apple apps, it's a powerful app with not a lot to it. There are only a handful of options. So let's talk about those options.

First, like a lot of Mac apps, this one can be run in full screen mode; just click the green button in the upper left corner. To exit full screen mode, you can either click the green button again or hit the ESC button on your keyboard. When you are using an app in full screen, you can always get back to your desktop by swiping with three fingers to your right on the Trackpad.

So that first photo was just for fun and now you want to get rid of it. That's really easy; on the bottom of the screen you'll see all of your recent photos. Click the one you want to delete, and hit the X in the corner.

But let's say you really like a photo—so much so that you want to share it with all of your friends. Just click the photo, and then hit the square button with an arrow pointing up, and pick how you want to share it.

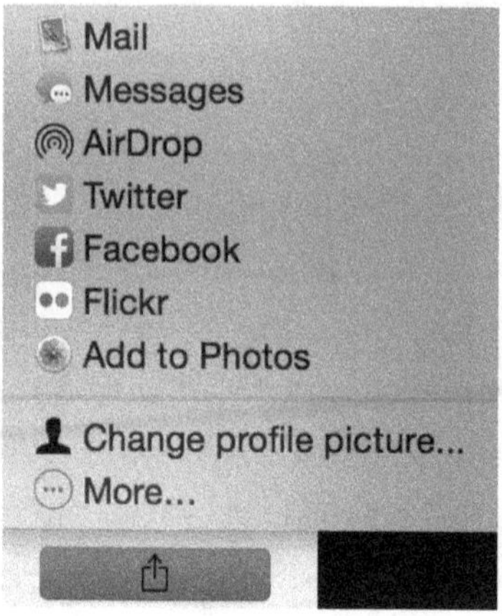

There are all sorts of effects for taking photos and videos. Try a few out; just click on the Effects button in the bottom right corner (Note: if you don't see that button then you probably are still viewing your photos, so click the camera button to get back).

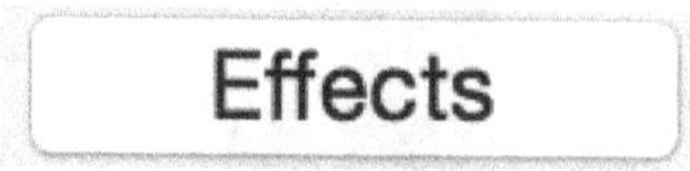

This will bring up 45 different camera effects.

You won't see all 45 at once; you'll see them nine at a time; click the arrows or the circles to see the next nine effects (Note: The last page of effects is for you to add your own backgrounds). When you see the effect you want, just click it.

When you are back to the main screen, there are three options in the lower left corner of the box.

The default box is the middle one. That takes one photo. The first one will take four different photos (one in each box), and the last will take a video of you. When using the video option, the camera will change to a video recorder.

If you want to use some of the fancier effects where it puts you somewhere you aren't (say Yosemite or the beach), then it will ask you to step out of the picture so it can detect the background;

then after a few seconds you will step back in. It's best to use a solid background for this effect. If you aren't happy with the way it looks, then you can reset the filter by going to the Menu bar on top, then clicking View and finally clicking Reset Effect.

If you want to add your own background, then go to the last page of Effects, and drag a photo of your choice into the box. Once you see that photo appear, click on it to activate the effect.

Don't be afraid to play around with the program. There's nothing you can press that will mess anything up!

CALENDAR

Calendar is another feature that can be synced to your iCloud account—so as long as you're using the same account, then everything you put in your calendar from your computer will also show up on your iPhone and iPad. You can also sync the calendar to other ones you may be using online like Google or Yahoo.

To get started with it, go to your Launchpad in the Dock and click on the Calendar icon.

At the top of the application window from left to right you have the standard stoplight buttons, Calendars, New Event (+), several different views including Day and Month, and the Search bar.

Syncing Calendars

If you already use a calendar with iCloud, Google, Yahoo, or any other provider, you can sync it up with the Mac Calendar application.

1. In the top menu bar click Calendar > Add Account.
2. Like you did with Mail, you'll be prompted to enter your name, email address, and password.

Once you finish the setup process your events from that calendar should automatically populate in the Calendar window. If you have multiple accounts with separate calendars, you can filter through them by clicking on the Calendars button in the toolbar, and checking or unchecking the boxes next to the appropriate calendars.

Changing Views

You can change the calendar view between Day, Week, Month, or Year by clicking on the corresponding button in the toolbar.

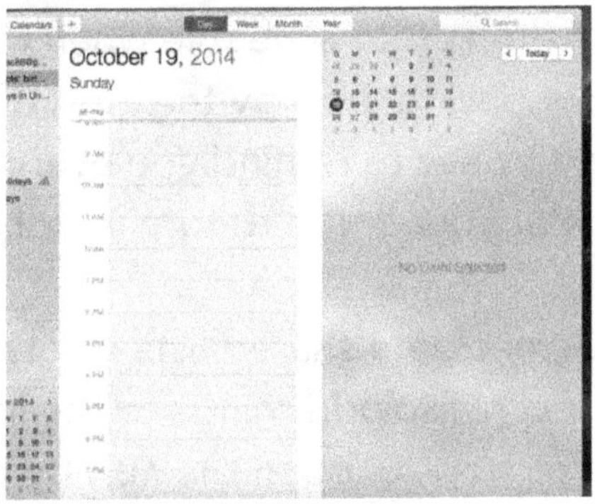

Day will display all of that day's events, broken down by hour.

Week will show you the whole week at a glance, and displays blocks for events so you can easily see when you have events, and if you have any upcoming free time.

The Month view will probably be your default view if you just need your calendar to remind you about bill payments and due dates, or don't have too many appointments each month but they are scattered through the month.

REMINDERS

As the name implies, the Reminders application is used to remind you of things—and, as you might have guessed by now, it can be synced using iCloud to the Reminders app on your iPhone or iPad.

The app lets you create lists for things like groceries or anything else on your mind; you can also use the app to schedule when things are due—like paying a bill by the 15th of the month. It can even be set to remind you every time you leave or arrive at your home to turn your home alarm on or off.

You can create shared lists so others in your network can also add things to the list.

To get started, open the app by clicking on the Launchpad icon, then selecting it from the list of apps.

Creating a list is still very simple. Tap Add List from the lower right corner of your screen.

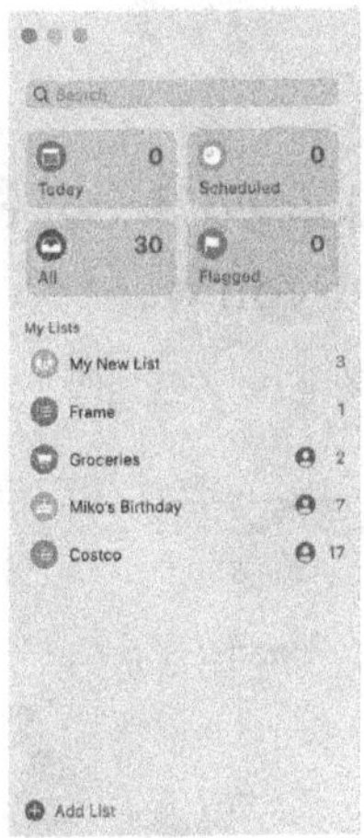

Once you create your first list, you can start adding to it by tapping the '+' button in the upper right corner. This lets you add the item as well as set when it's due and even include images and attachments.

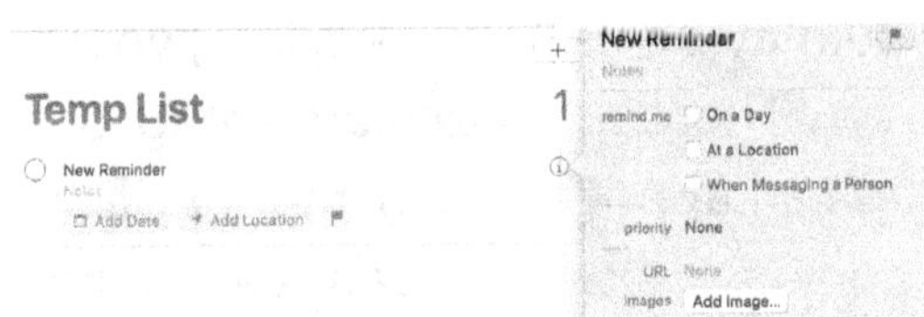

If you tap the ⓘ at any point, you'll be able to add more details (such as a due date or even what location to remind you at—you could, for example, have it remind you when you get to the grocery store).

Tap Return on your keyboard to add another item.

To share a list, right-click (two-finger click) the name and add a person that you want to share it with.

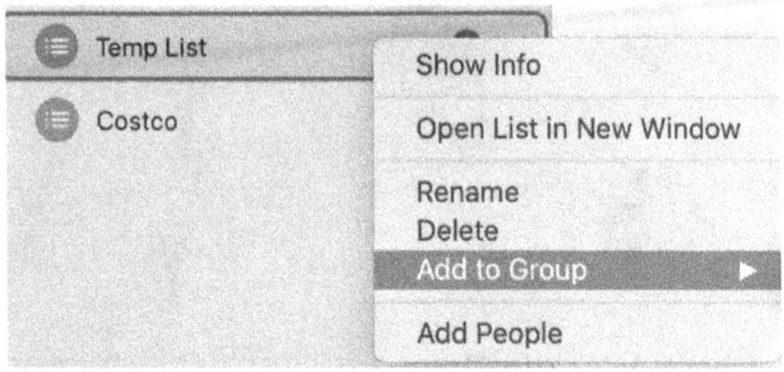

This option also works to remove a list.

Mail

You may be used to checking your email in your browser. There are a few advantages to emailing through an app. One is instant notifications when mail comes; another is features you might not get in browser-based mail.

If you want to try an app, then there are plenty you can choose from: Airmail, Outlook, Spark, Canary Mail (some are free, some are not).

For this book, I'm going to cover only one app: Apple Mail.

MAIL CRASH COURSE

To get started, go to your Launchpad and click the Mail app.

Next, it will ask you to sign into your email provider. The steps vary depending on the services you use, but it will walk you through each step.

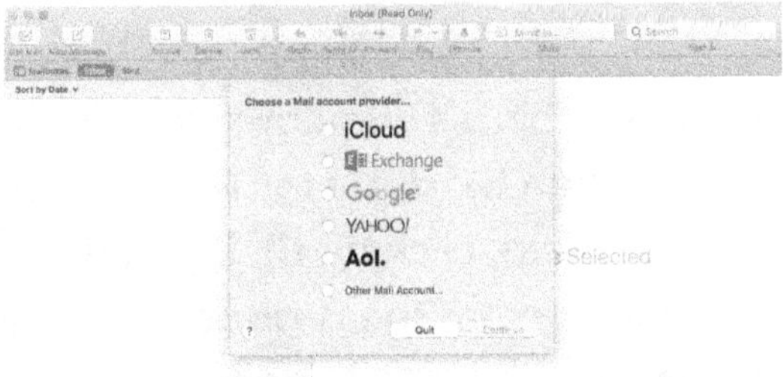

Once you have your mail set up, you'll immediately start seeing your inbox fill up with all the messages from that account. Don't see it? Go to "Get New Mail" under Mailbox in the top menu.

The app should look pretty familiar to you because most the features from your browser mail are there.

A few features you should know about:

Block – If there's someone you don't want to hear from, then block them. To do so, open the email from them, click on their name, and select Block Contact from the dropdown. If only blocking people in real-life was that easy!

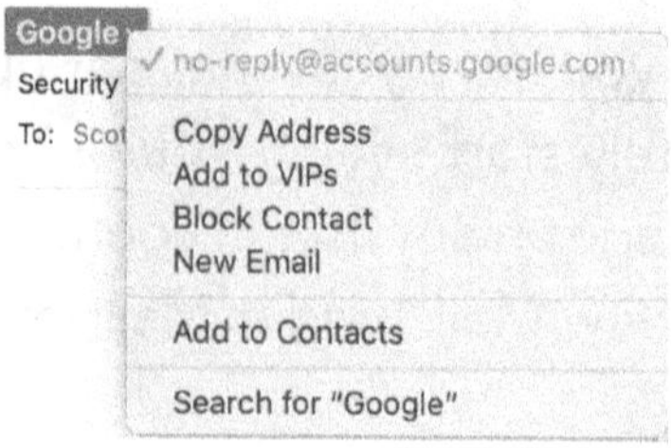

When you right-click (two-finger click) on a mail message, you also have a few options.

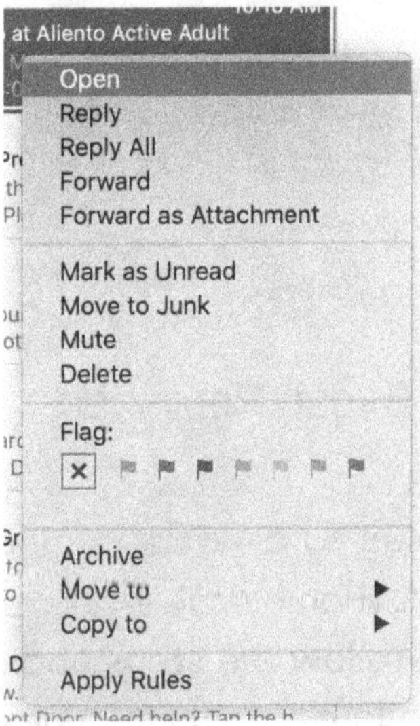

If you have ever used email before, then you will know what Reply, Reply All, etc., do. One that might be new is "Flag." Flag lets you color coordinate different messages to help you find them more easily.

You can also right-click (two-finger click) in the side menu to get more options.

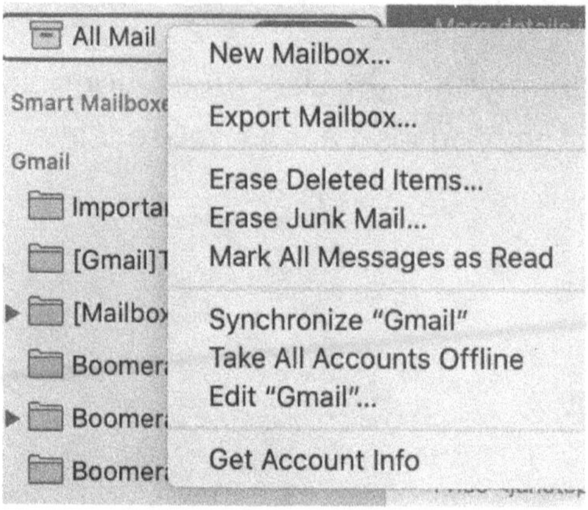

Location Based Reminder

If you want to create a reminder that is location-based (i.e. "when I leave work, remind me to call wife") then follow the steps above.

Click the Information icon next to the reminder (the "i" with a circle).

This will bring up a few extra options. One says, "remind me" with a checkbox for "At a location"; click that checkbox. Next, enter the address, and select if you want the reminder when you get there or when you're leaving there.

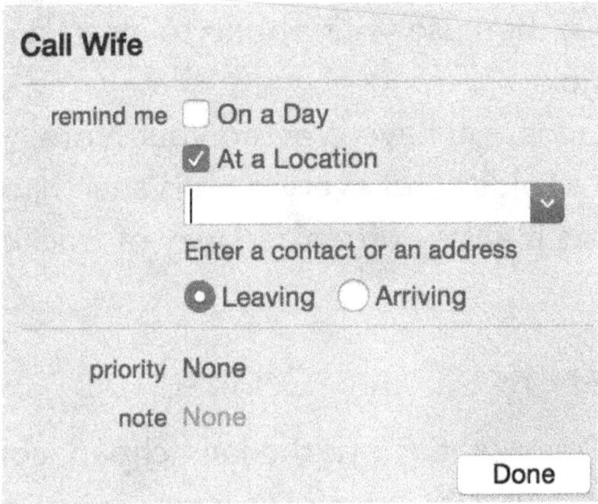

WELCOME TO NOTE TAKING 2.0

If you are new to Apple, then the obvious question on your mind might be: why Notes? What is it good for and when should you use it?

Notes is probably *not* what you want to use to write this year's Christmas Newsletter or create a flier for your lost puppy; Notes really excels when you want to create a shared list, jot down school notes, or do something that doesn't need a lot of formatting.

Notes really shines when you sync it with your iPhone; with your iPhone sync'd, you can write your notes, then use your phone to insert a sketch or image.

Once you have created your Note, you can add it to a folder and everything is searchable, which makes it a very organized way of tracking things.

The Notes Crash Course

To open it, go to the Launchpad icon on your Dock and click the Notes icon.

Notes, like most of the apps in Catalina, syncs to your iPhone and iPad as long as you are logged into the same iCloud account.

Unlike word processing editors that you may be used to, there is no fancy ribbon or menu bar with lots of features. There's a side bar with a list of all your notes (across devices if you use an iPhone / iPad sync'd to your Mac).

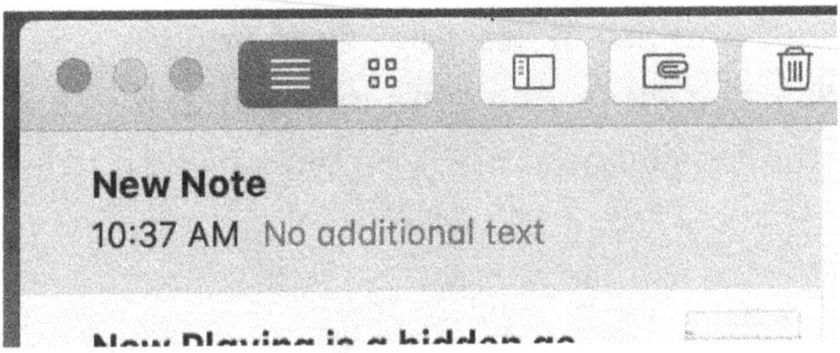

On the top is a very basic menu bar.

Views

The first option next to the app resize options (the red / yellow / green dots) is the view toggle.

This toggle switches between a list view of your notes and a thumbnail view (see below).

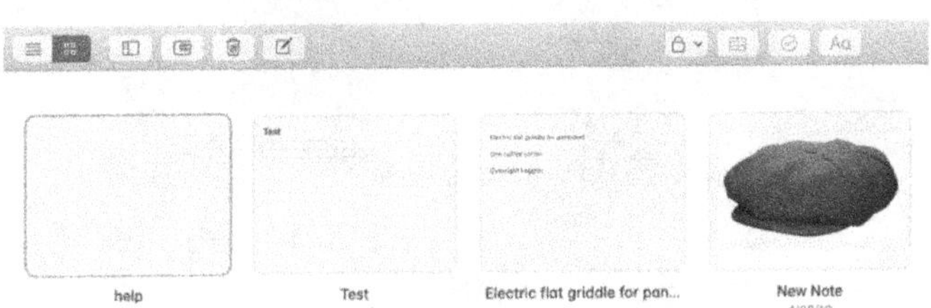

If you are in list view, then you only need to click the Note one time to open it; if you are in thumbnail view, then you will need to double click it.

Folders

The next button is for creating folders.

This brings up a list of all your folders (if any).

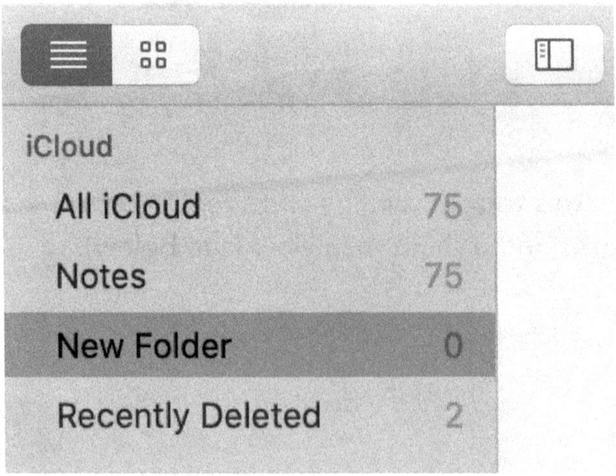

If you don't have one yet, then click New Folder at the bottom of the window.

To rename, delete, or add people to the folder, click the three dots with the circle around them.

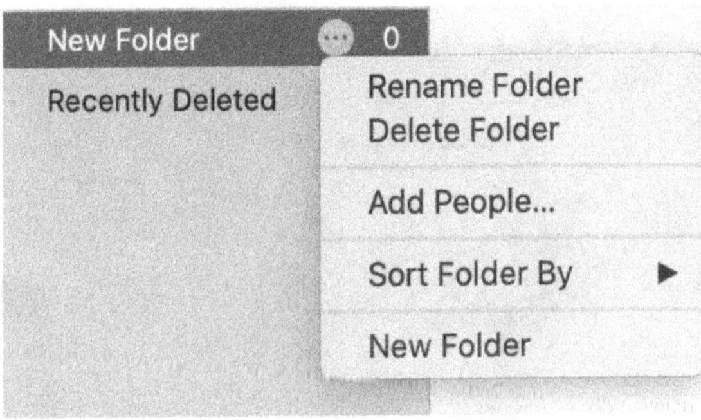

Finally, to add a note to a folder, click it from the side, and then drag it into the desired folder.

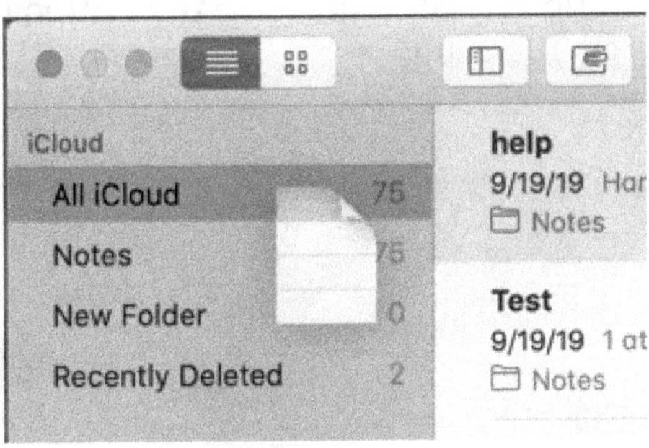

Once you are done, click the view button again to hide the folders panel.

Viewing Attachments

The next option looks like the button to attach things; that's not correct. It's the option to view all the attachments you have added into notes. When you click on it, you can sort by all the different attachment types (Photos & Videos, Scans, Maps, Websites, Audio, and Documents)

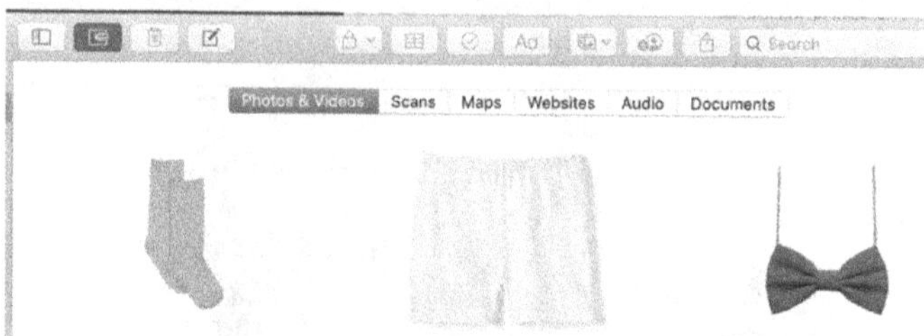

When you double click an attachment, it opens a preview of it (it does *not* open the note which it's found in). If you would like to see the Note that it is in, then right click to bring up the option menu and click "Show in Note."

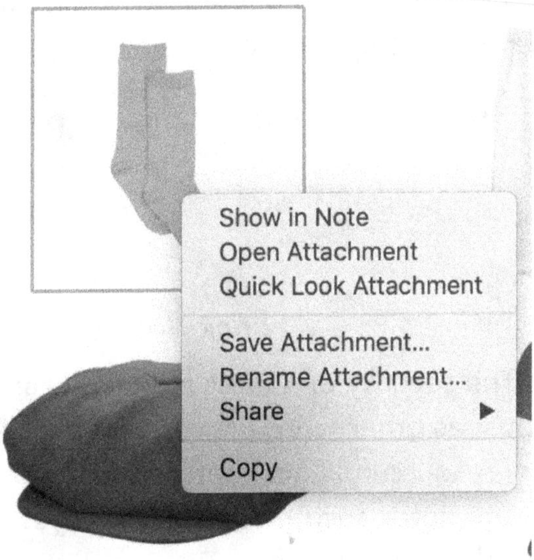

Delete Note

The next option is pretty straightforward. It deletes the note that you have currently selected.

Creating a Note

Next to the delete button is the "Create a Note" button, which, as you can expect, creates a note. When you open your note, the left panel will have the name of the note with a time stamp, and the right will have an empty text area to write in. The title of the note will change once you start typing text; the first line of text is the title of your note. You cannot rename the title; if you change the first line of text in the note, then the title is changed automatically.

Lock Note

The security on Notes may not seem quite as robust as other word processors, but there is a very resourceful Lock feature that helps keep private notes secure and for your eyes only. To use it, click the Lock icon.

This will bring up a dialog box that asks you to add a password. Now anytime you want to open the Note, you'll need a password. If you forget your password then you will not be able to access your Note, so be careful!

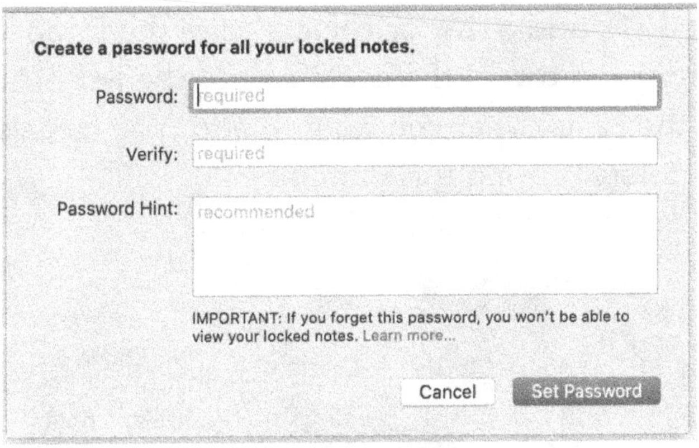

Create a Table

You can also add Tables to your Note. Personally, I would stick to adding tables into other word processing suites, because this is one feature a bit more cumbersome than other tools out there. But if you want to try it out, click the Tables icon.

This adds a very small table to your note—just two rows and two columns.

To add a row or column, click the three little dots on top of the column or to the left of the row, then click what you want to add. You can also delete it using this method.

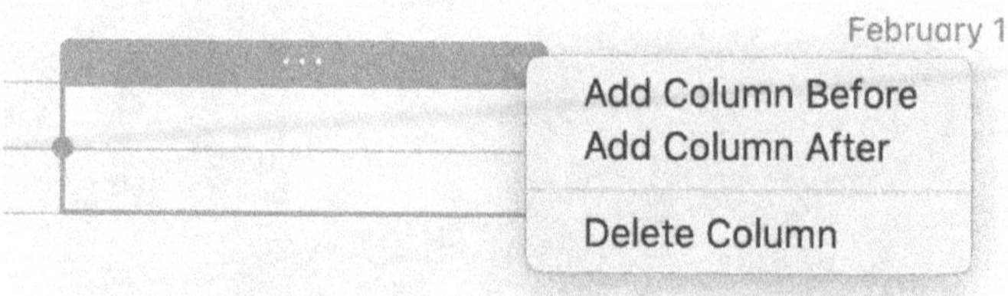

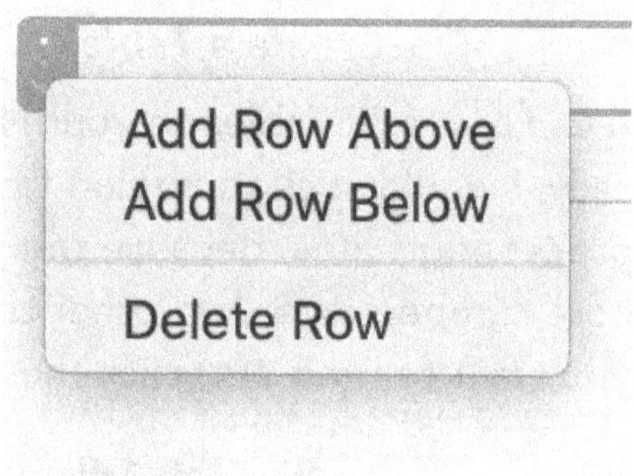

Create a Checklist

If you are using Notes to create a shared list between people (or just a list for yourself), click the Check icon.

This turns each line of text into a list. Hitting return on your keyboard will create a new list item; hitting return twice will take it out of list mode and return it to normal typing.

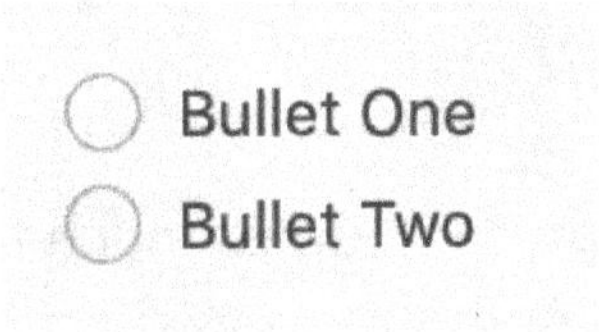

You can click inside any of the circles and check an item off. If you made a mistake, then just uncheck it again.

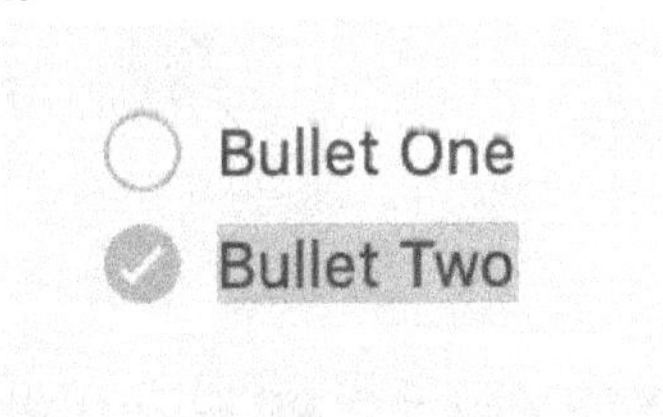

You can also move a list item up or down by right clicking it, then going to "Move List Item."

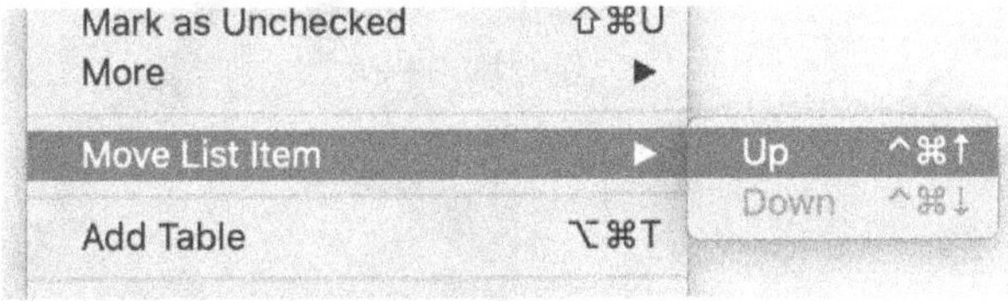

By right clicking, you can also go to More and check off all items (or uncheck all items).

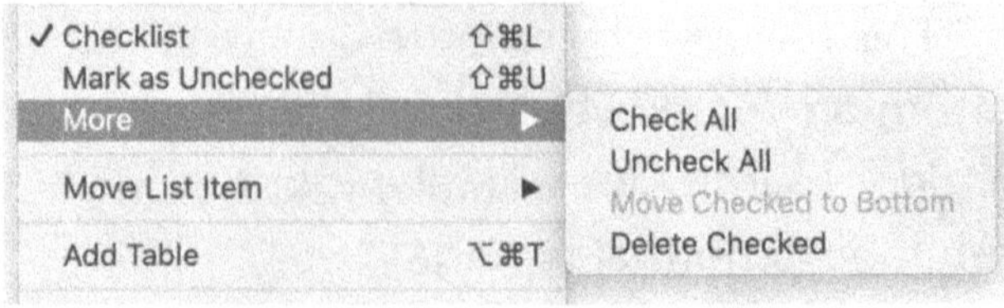

Add a Style

While you can't do as much to the format as you could in other word processors, Notes does have basic styles. To access them, click the Aa icon.

This gives you a drop-down of all the possible styles available.

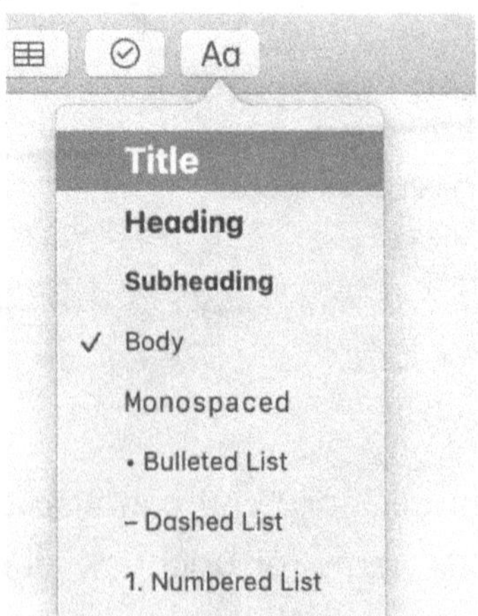

Adding Sketches and Images

One of the many areas Apple has always really shined is with syncing between devices. Using Notes for Mac with your iPhone, you can add in sketches or take photos.

To get started, go to the photos icon. This brings down a drop down of all your options. You can, of course, add any photo on your Mac with the Photos option.

Using the next three options (Take Photo, Scan Documents, Add Sketch) will bring up an image that asks you to connect to your phone to complete the tasks (make sure you are on the same network).

When you add a sketch, you draw it on your phone.

Once you hit done on your phone, it will automatically appear in Notes for Mac.

Adding Collaborators

If you want to add others to your note, click the icon with the person and +.

Next click "Note 'New Note'".

It will ask how you want to add them. Through messages, a link, AirDrop, etc.

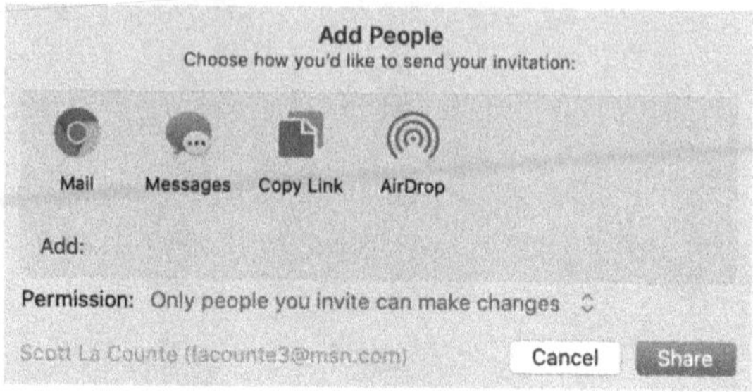

When you're ready, click share, but before you do, click the Permissions drop-down and make sure it's set up the way you want. You can either let the note be view-only for others or you can let them make changes.

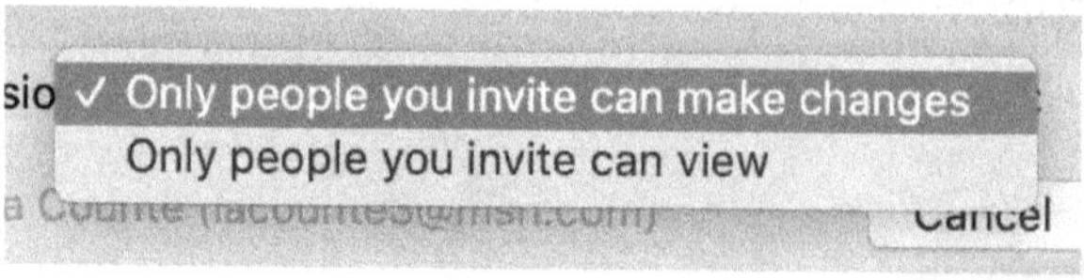

Sharing Notes

If you want to share the note without adding the person to the note, click the share icon.

Next, pick how you would like to share the note.

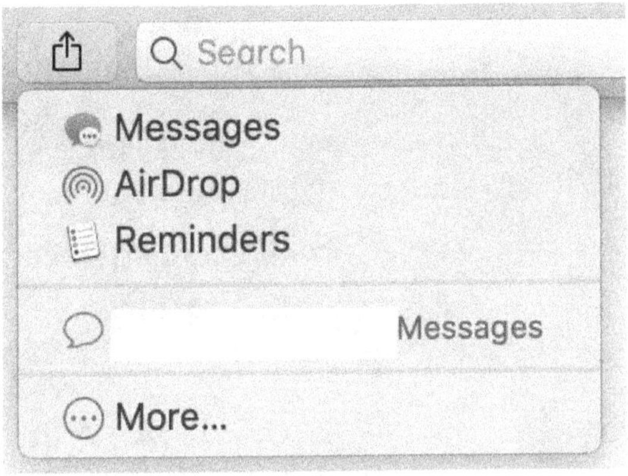

Searching Notes

The last option on the toolbar is the search box. This lets you search all of your notes for different keywords. For example, whenever I go somewhere with a public Wi-Fi, I add the network key to a Wi-Fi password note (I don't recommend this for sensitive passwords); whenever I need to quickly find it, I search for "WiFi" and it comes up immediately.

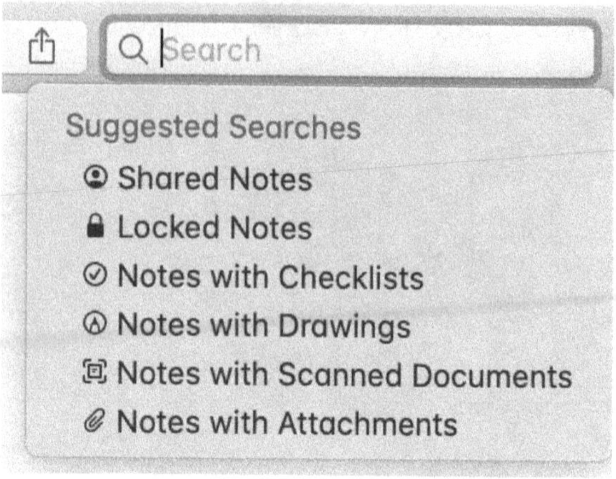

Exporting Notes

Now that we've seen all the features on the toolbar, let's go up one level to the top menu bar. Everything you did in the toolbar, you can also do there; there are also, however, a few extra features.

The first is exporting a Note as a PDF. That's found under File > Export as PDF.

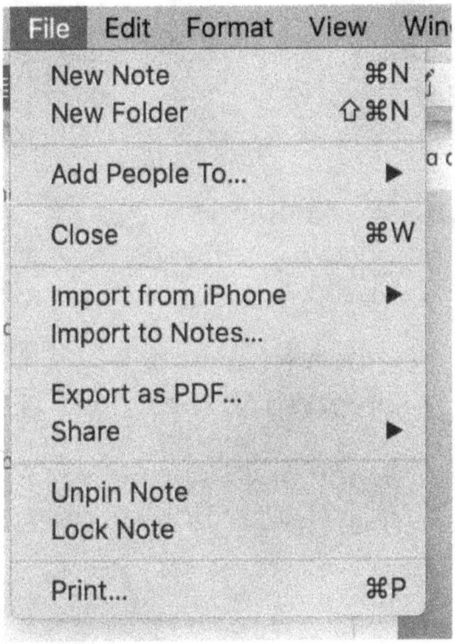

Above Export is the Import option; personally, I find it easier just to share a note from another device, but if you have a copy somewhere and have a reason to import it, then you would go here.

Pinning Notes

Pinning notes is a very basic, but useful feature; when you click on a note and then select to Pin it from File > Pin Note, it sticks it at the top of all your notes to make it easier to find.

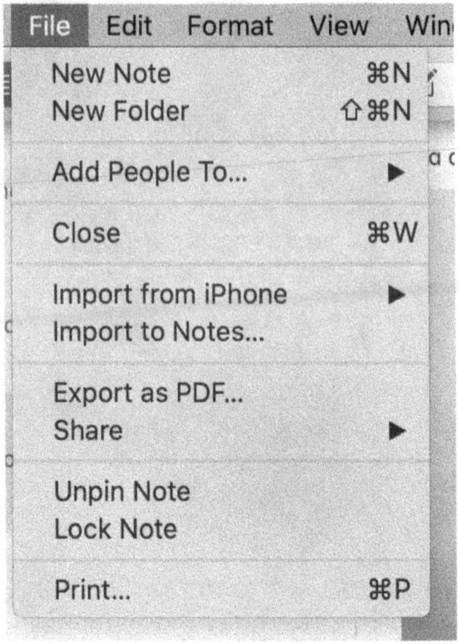

Attaching Files

Unlike many word processing apps, you can actually attach files to Notes. Go to Edit > Attach File.

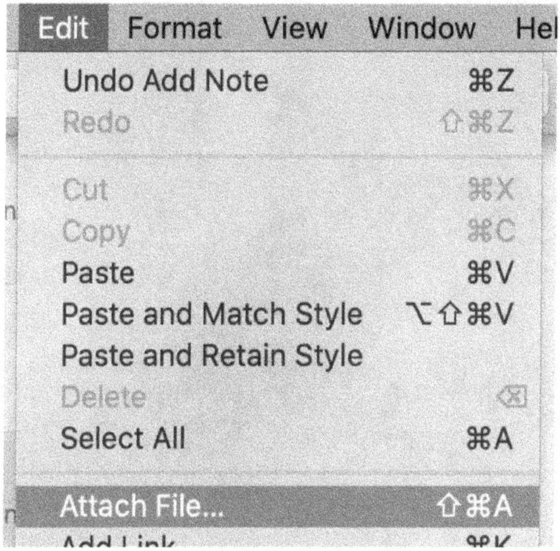

Spell Check

Like any word processing software, there is a spell checker buried in the top menu. You can start spell check by going to Edit > Spelling and Grammar. By default, it checks spelling / grammar as you type.

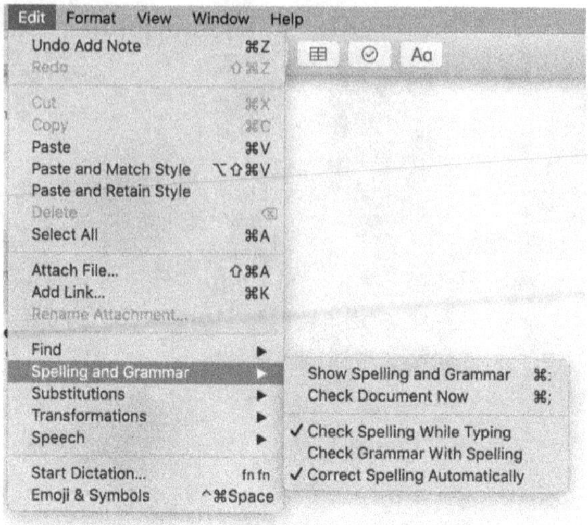

Font Formatter

Finally, while changing the font color / type is not quite as simple as Pages or Word, it is still possible. Go to Format > Font.

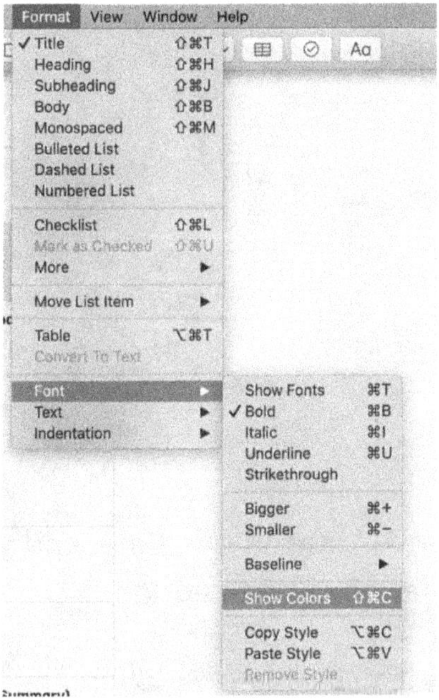

IPHONE NOTES

Now that you know your way around Notes, let's look at how it works on the iPad (which is almost identical to how it looks on the iPhone).

In terms of functionality, everything is almost exactly the same. The difference is just where things are located.

At first glance, Notes looks basically the same as it always has. Notice that little plus sign above the keyboard? That's what's different.

Tap the '+' button one time, and you'll see the options that have been added.

Starting from the left side is a checkmark, which is what you press if you'd like to make a checklist instead of a note. For each new checkmark, just tap the return button on the keyboard.

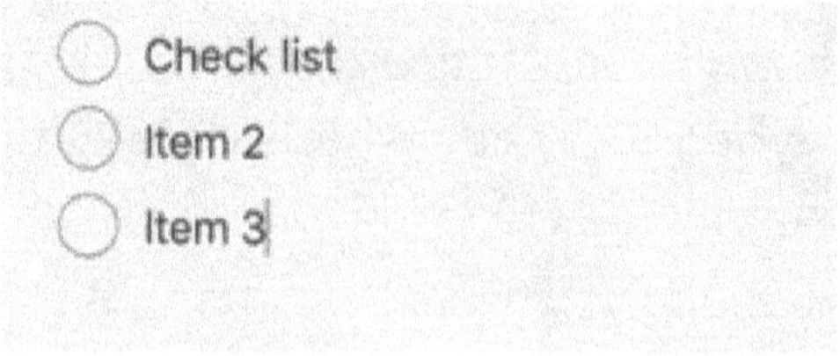

The 'Aa' button is what you would press if you would like to format the note a little (larger fonts, bold, bulleted text, etc.).

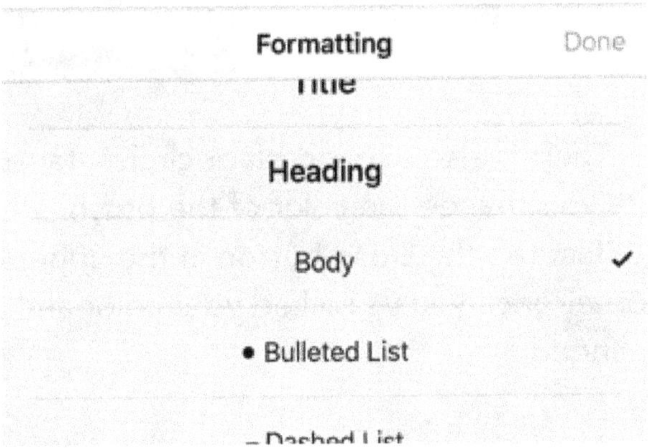

The little camera button will let you add a photo you have taken, or let you take a photo from within the app and insert it.

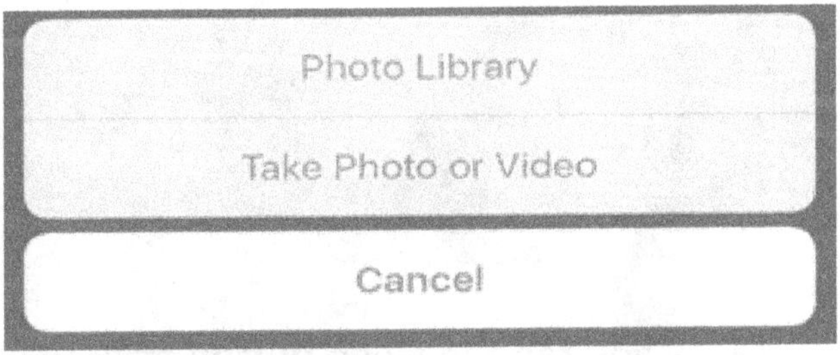

And finally, the squiggly line lets you draw in the Notes app; when you press it, you'll see three different brushes (pen, marker, and pencil) which each work a little differently, as well as a ruler and eraser. This is really the biggest difference in Notes in iOS; unlike the Mac, Notes in iOS lets you draw on your screen—something you can do on your Mac only by syncing to your iPhone or iPad.

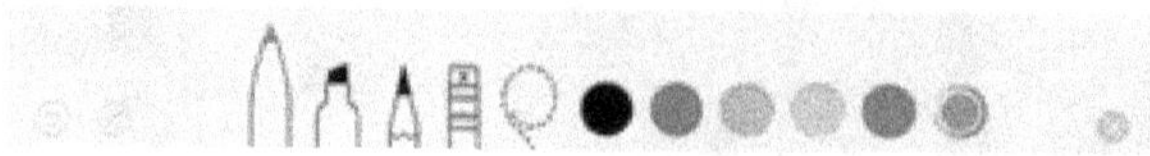

There's also a round black circle—tapping that lets you change the color of the brush.

Just tap the Done button in the upper right corner once you've picked your color and it will be changed.

Once you tap the Done button after you've finished drawing, you will go back to the note. If you tap the drawing, however, it will activate it again and you can make changes or add to your drawing.

It's obviously not the most advance drawing app—but that's the point—it's not supposed to be. As the name of the app says, this app is just for jotting or drawing quick notes.

In the Settings menu a Search option has been added at the top. There are a lot of Settings in iOS and there are more and more with each update—Search Settings let you quickly access the setting you want. So, for instance, if you want to stop getting notifications for a certain app, you no longer have to thumb through endless apps—now just search for it.

Notes has also been added to Safari, so if you want to add a website to a note, it's now possible.

Whenever you see the option to use Markup you will be using the Notes interface.

iTunes In a Non-iTunes World

iTunes is a thing on Windows. It's where you buy and manage music, shows and all things content that you bought from Apple. On a Mac? It used to be a thing. In Catalina OS, however, Apple has pulled iTunes apart and made it separate—so if you want to buy music, you now go to Apple Music; if you want to buy videos, you go to Apple TV. The interface is very simple.

I'll cover Apple Music more in the chapter on Apple Services. In this section I'll cover only how to buy music and iTunes Match.

Show the iTunes Store in Apple Music

When you open the Music app, you should see an option in the left menu for the iTunes Store.

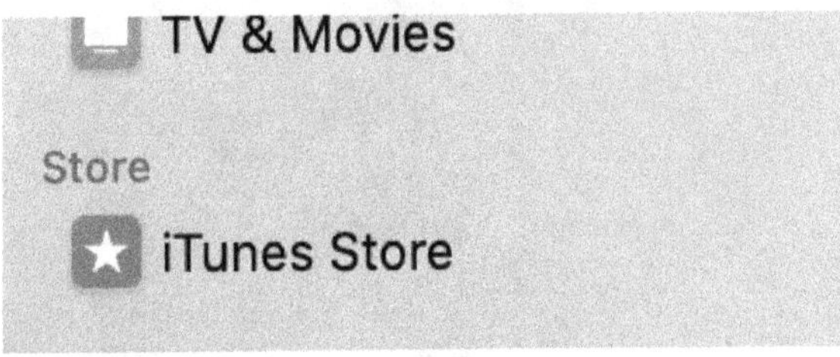

When you click on that, it will show you an iTunes Store that looks a lot like the old iTunes app—nearly identical to the one you might be used to if you have an iPad or iPhone.

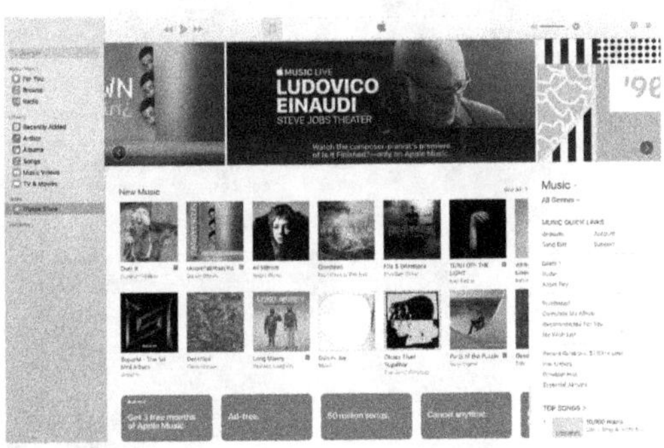

If you have an Apple Music subscription, then there's a chance that iTunes Store link will be missing—why buy an album if it comes with your subscription, after all? Just because you have a subscription to listen to music for free doesn't mean you won't want to buy anything. If you want to buy an album but don't see the link, then here's what you do:

Go to File > Preferences...

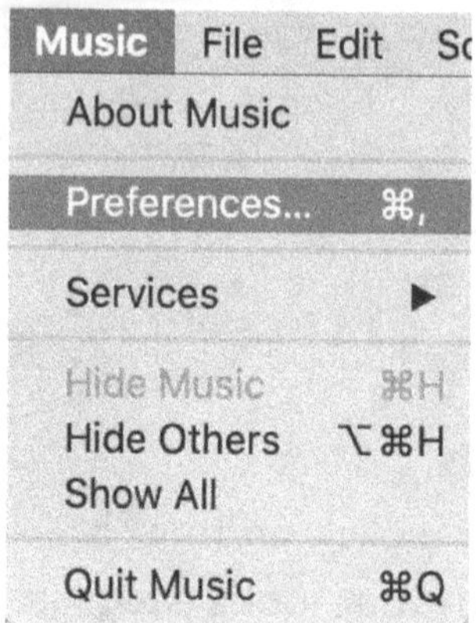

Under the General tab, check off iTunes Store.

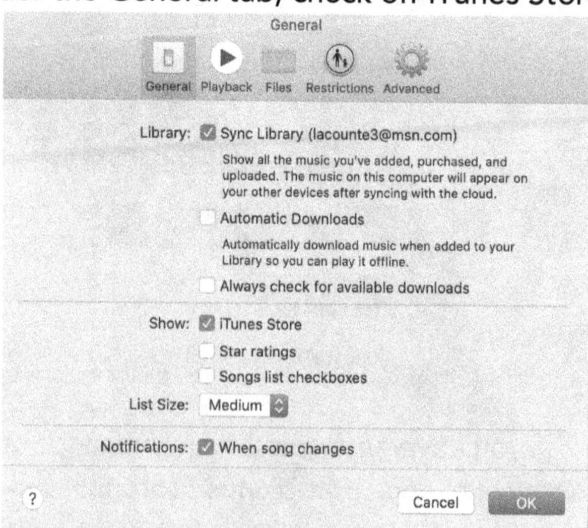

After hitting OK, it will show up in your left menu.

How does the store work? Clicking on the Search bar in the top right-hand corner will pull up trending searches in case you are looking for what's hot. If you are looking for a specific song or movie, type it into the Search bar and iTunes will load it for you. Scroll through the main page and the latest releases will be shown front and center, letting you see new music at a glance.

On the right side of the screen you will see Music in big letters, with All Genres under It. Clicking the All Genres link opens a dropdown menu with every main genre you can think of.

The big Music link will open a dropdown menu with the rest of the iTunes store options: Movies, TV Shows, App Store, Books, Podcasts, Audiobooks, and iTunes U. Go through each one and you will see that they all follow the same conventions as the Music page, with charts, top downloads, and new releases.

To purchase new music (or any other media) that interests you, use either the Search bar or browse through the categories to find what you're looking for. When you reach a song or album you'd like, click it to bring up the full information menu for that item.

The window will display all types of information including album price, individual song price, track list, audio previews, release date, ratings, reviews, and similar items. To buy the album (or a single song), click on the price; a prompt window will come up to make sure you really wanted to buy that album, and you can continue by clicking the blue Buy button.

If you already have funds in your iTunes account, or have a card on file, the purchase will be made and the song(s) will begin to automatically download. If you don't have any money in the account, or haven't yet added a payment method, you will be asked to enter that information before the purchase can be made.

After your purchases are fully downloaded, you'll be able to enjoy your new music by clicking on the My Music tab and selecting your latest addition.

iTunes Match

Apple Music is a great service, but if you already have an extensive music library and don't want new music, then iTunes Match might be a solution for you.

iTunes Match is also great if you have a large music library but don't have enough storage on your phone.

Signing up for Match will allow you to store your entire collection on iCloud, including music that you've ripped from CDs and didn't purchase through iTunes. This way you'll be able to stream your entire library from any Apple device connected to iCloud without taking up any storage.

The songs are "matched" by Apple's online music database, so when you are playing the song on your iPhone, for example, it isn't actually the same file that you uploaded or purchased. Rather, it's Apple's version of the song in full 256 Kbps, even if the song you originally uploaded or purchased was of lower audio quality. If the song is not found on Apple's own servers (your cousin's Whitesnake cover band perhaps), it will playback the original file you uploaded, with the original audio quality.

Unfortunately, iTunes Match isn't free. If you'd like to sign up for it, expect to pay $24.99 for a yearly subscription.

App Store

The App Store is where you'll be able to download and install many different applications that have been developed specifically for use with a Mac computer. These apps will do everything from add new functionalities and make your life easier, to providing a fun way to waste time and play some games during downtime at work. Keep in mind that for the App Store to be functional, you need to be connected to the Internet.

To be clear, apps purchased on the App Store only run on Macs; if you have two Macs, you can download it on both if you have the same account. But you cannot download them on your iPhone or iPad. So, if you are wondering why a game you downloaded on the iPhone or iPad is not available free on your Mac, that's why. Mac apps are developed using an entirely different framework.

Open the App Store by selecting it either through the Dock or Launchpad. The App Store's home page will greet you, showing you the latest and greatest in the world of apps.

At the top you will see different sections: Featured, Top Charts, Categories, Purchases, and Updates.

The Featured, Top Charts, and Categories tabs will show you apps that can be downloaded, but organized in different ways. Featured will show you Best New Apps, Best New Games, Editor's Choices, and collections of different apps that work great together.

Top Charts shows you the best of the best when it comes to available apps, and is broken down by Top Paid, Top Free, and Top Grossing. On the right side, you can also browse through Top Apps broken down by category, in case you wanted to refine your search.

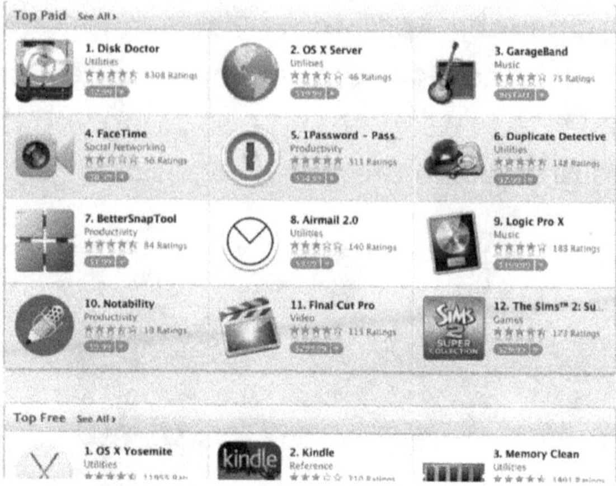

Categories further breaks down your app hunting into different categories like Business, Education, Reference, Productivity, Medical, Entertainment, and Games.

Choosing a category will bring up more selections and the right side will be filled with even more categories. For example, selecting the

Business category will bring you to the main Business apps page where the hottest apps are listed. On the right side, smaller categories like Apps for Writers, App Development, or Apps for Designers can be selected. It doesn't matter what category of apps you are currently under; the list remains the same in the right half.

Purchases and Updates are where you can go to view past App Store downloads. The Purchases title can be a bit misleading, because your free apps will also appear here. In the Updates section, you can view which apps need to be updated to the latest version. If you have multiple apps that need updating, you can choose the Update All button and it will go down the entire list.

PHOTOS

Photos has been around on the Mac for quite a while. In OS Catalina, however, it got a bit of a facelift that closer resembles the experience on the iPad and iPhone.

To get started, go to Photos from the Launchpad.

If your Mac is synced to your iPhone, then your photos are synced as well. No need to move them over. If you don't have an iPhone or you have other photos that you'd like to add that weren't taken on an Apple device, then you can go to File > Import.

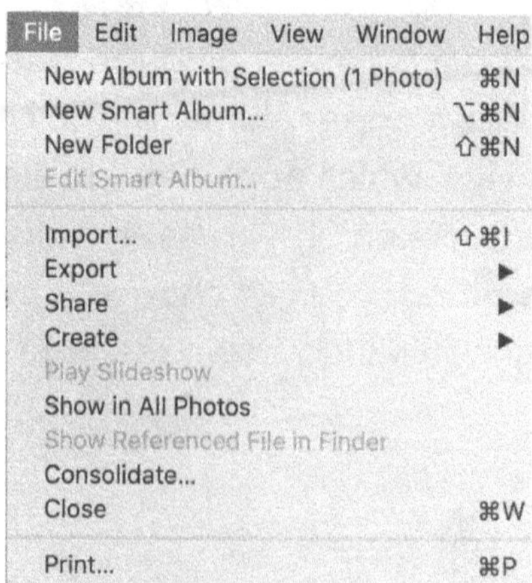

There are a few options to check out in the top menu. The first is the bigger / smaller slider.

This lets you adjust the thumbnail preview size of your photos.

Next to that is the Years / Months / Days / All Photos option, which lets you pick how photos are grouped.

If you have a photo selected, you can click the "i" and see information about the photo (what camera was used, resolution, ISO, file size, and more).

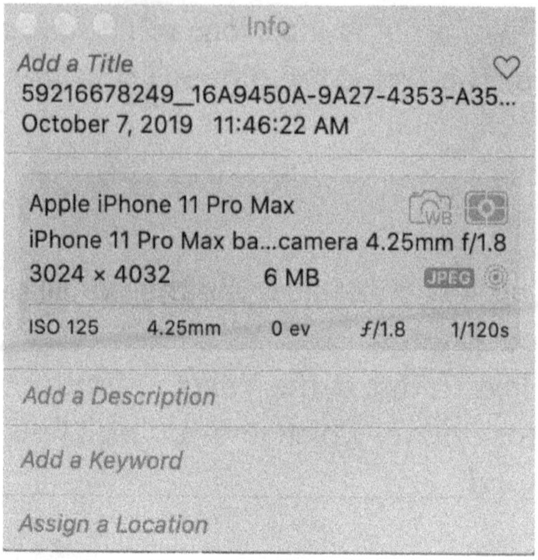

Next to information is the option to share, favorite, rotate, or search for images.

Search is pretty smart—you can search by the names of people or by the location it was taken.

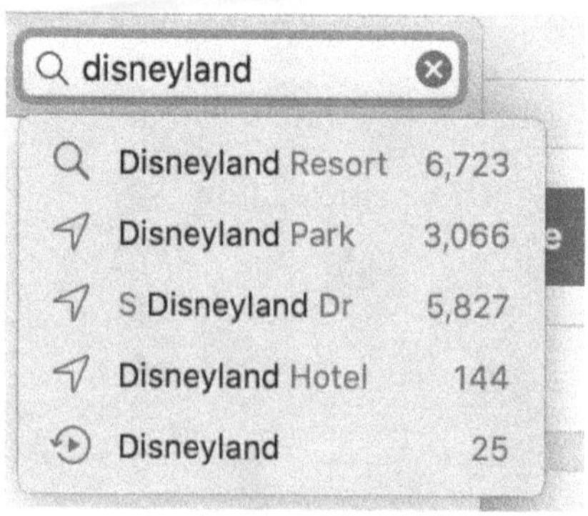

On the left menu, you have the option to view specific photos—photos with people, for example.

If you go into Memories, you can watch slideshows of past photos (Apple's AI groups these together). To watch the slideshow, right-click (two-finger click) on the memory you want to see.

Under Albums in the left menu, you can right-click to create a new Album.

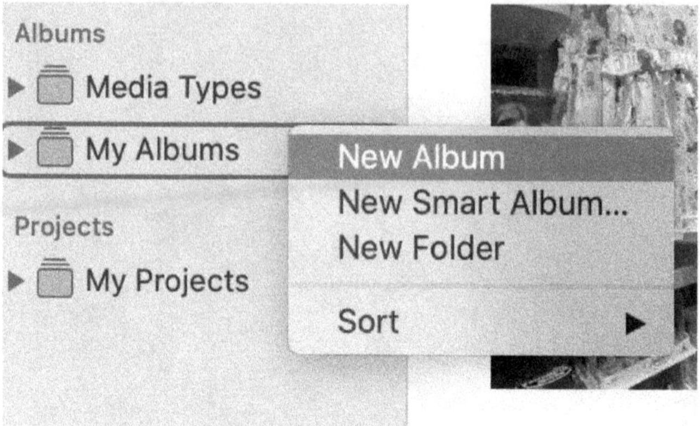

If you select New Smart Album, then you can create an Album based on a defined filter you select.

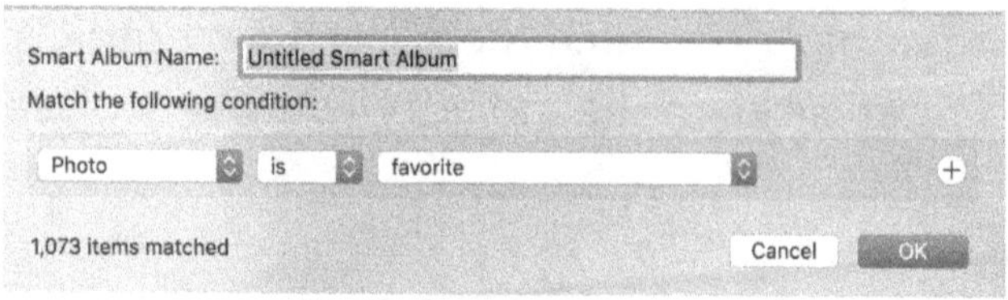

Once you create an Album, then you can right-click on any photo and add it to that Album.

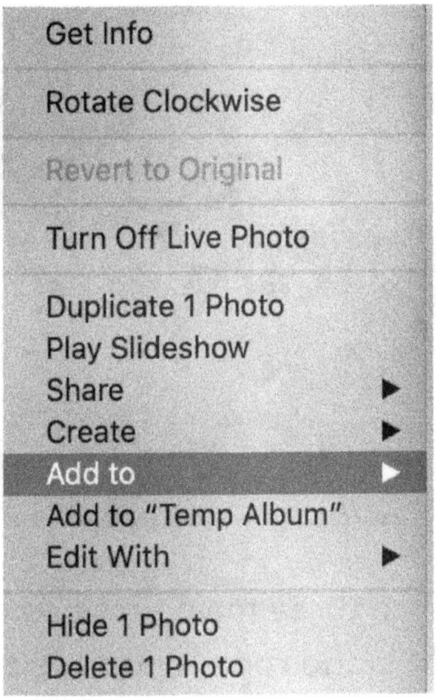

When you double-click on any photo, you can edit it. In edit mode, there's an option to auto edit, which adjust the lighting based on what the AI thinks is correct.

There are dozens of basic and advanced editing options.

There are three main sections when doing edits (accessible in the top menu): Adjust (lighting corrections), Filters (pre-defined photo filters), and Crop.

LESSER USED APPS

There are a lot of apps on Mac that you probably see but don't use. Here's a rundown of some of those apps and when you might use them.

TextEdit is Apple's answer to Microsoft's Notepad. This is a simple plain-text editor. It's certainly not fancy, but it's good for jotting down notes.

Stickies is a love it or hate it sort of app. If you're in the love it camp, though, they're still there. Stickies are like Post-it notes for your desktop. Just open the Stickies app from Launchpad and start sticking away!

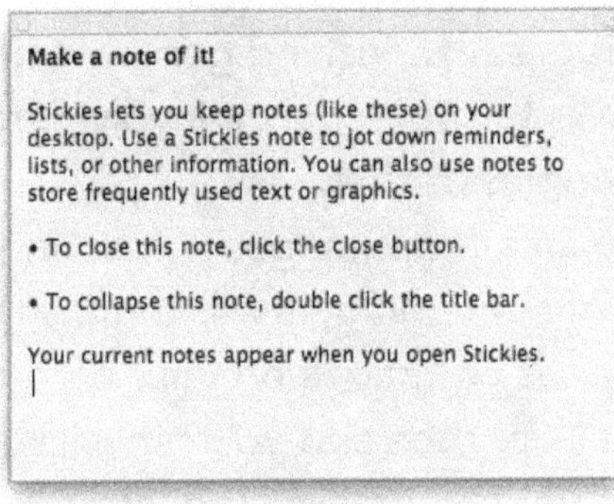

SIRI

If you've used Siri on the iPhone, iPad or Apple Watch, then you'll be right at home with this feature. Siri is built into the Dock. To use it, just click the Dock icon.

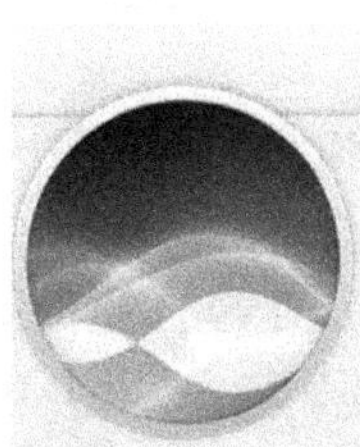

HINT: There's a shortcut key for bringing up Siri: hold the Command key and Spacebar.

Siri is great for asking general questions, but it also works for doing more involved tasks. Here's a few examples of that:

Drag and Drop Images – Ask Siri to find you photos of something; it will confirm if you want web images or images on your hard drive. It will bring back photos and you can click and drag them into documents, emails, and lots of other things.

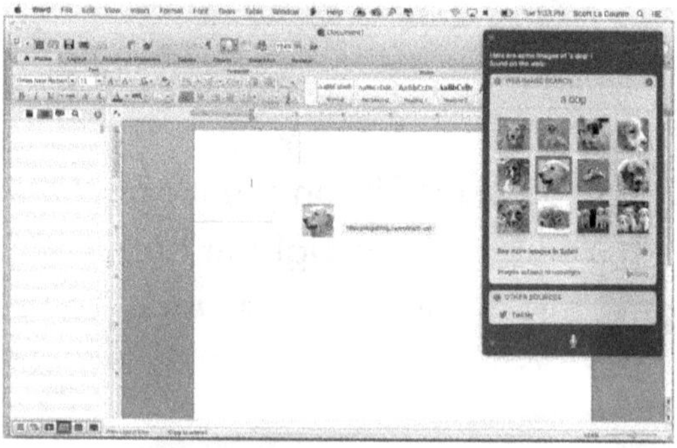

Locating Files – Siri works much like the finder...except easier. You can tell Siri to find a specific file, or you can tell Siri to find you all files opened last week, or virtually anything else.

Personal Assistant – Siri is great at doing tasks for you. You can ask Siri to email someone, read text messages, or make an appointment in your calendar. Just ask and see what happens!

If you'd like to change Siri's settings (change the voice from female to male, for example), then go to the Launchpad, open System Preferences, then click Siri.

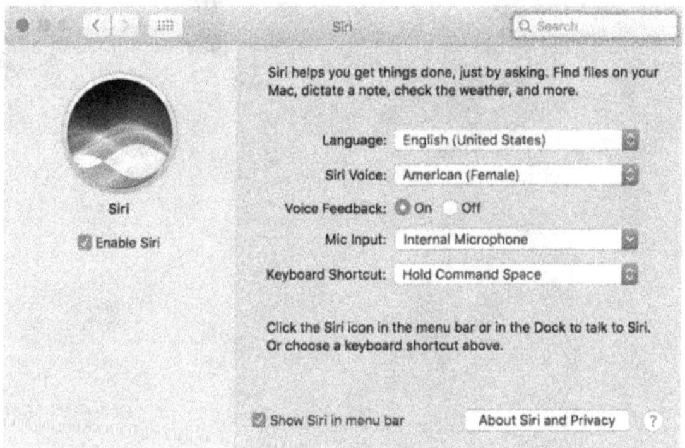

MacOS Meet iOS

The line between MacOS and iOS gets smaller with each update, and that trend continues with Catalina. The idea is that the apps you use on iOS should look the same on MacOS, so if you know how to use it in one place, you'll know how to use it in the other.

There are four apps in particular: News, Stock, Home, and Voice Memos.

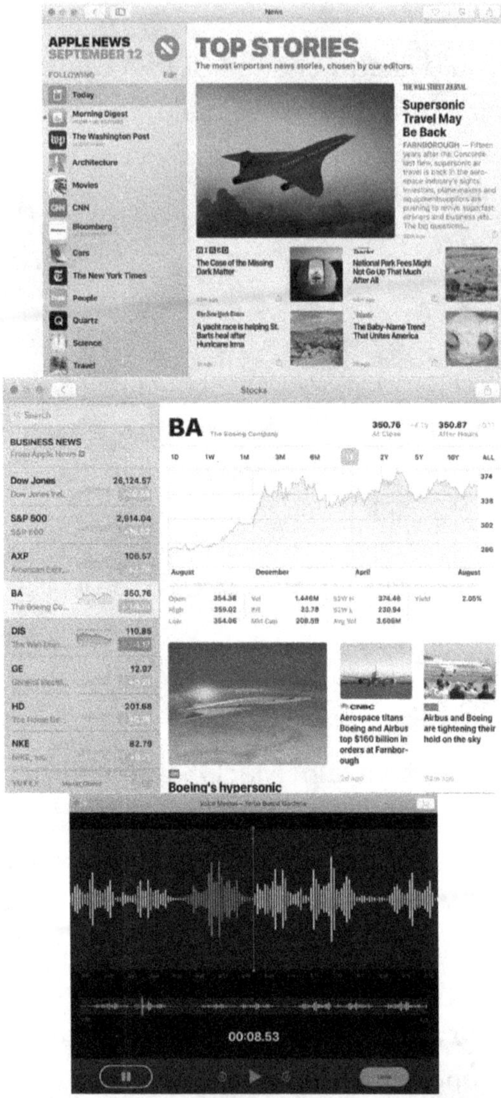

You can access these apps through the sidebar. Most of these apps will be self-explanatory. Home might be a little new to you, however. Apple has made a strong push on the Home with what it calls HomeKit. Developers can use HomeKit to develop home automation (turn the lights off from your phone sort of thing). If you have a HomePod (the fancy Siri speaker), this is where you would manage that.

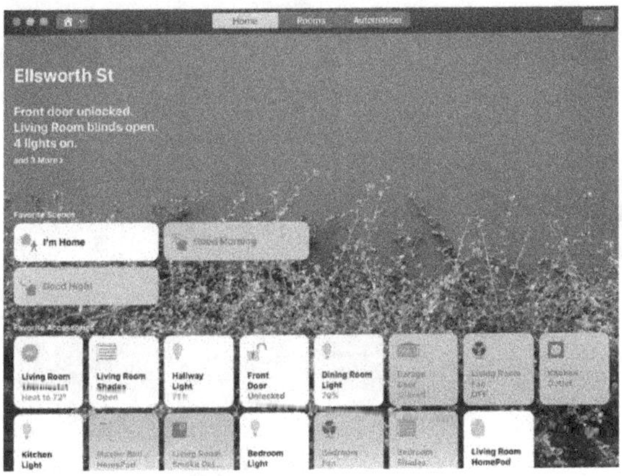

[7] Apple Services

This chapter will cover:

- iCloud
- Apple TV+
- Apple Music
- Apple News

Introduction

It used to be a few times a year Apple would take the stage and announce something that everyone's head exploded over! The iPhone! The iPad! The Apple Watch! The iPod!

That still happens today, but Apple also is well aware of the reality: most people don't upgrade to new hardware every year. How does a company make money when that happens? In a word: services.

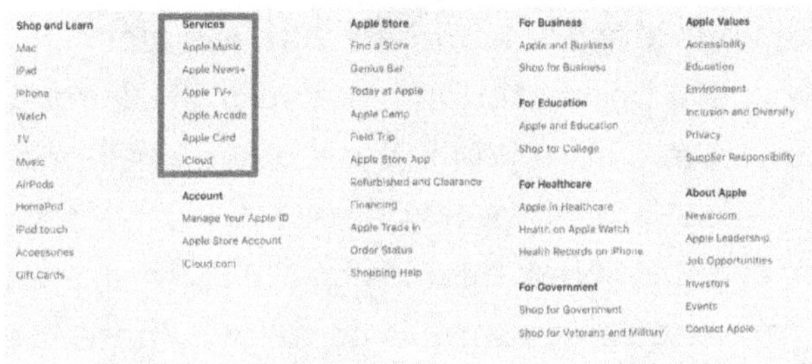

In the past few years (especially in 2019) Apple announced several services—things people would opt into to pay for monthly. It was a way to continue making money even when people were not buying hardware.

For it to work, Apple knew they couldn't just offer a subpar service and expect people to pay because it said Apple. It had to be good. And it is!

iCloud

iCloud is something that Apple doesn't talk a lot about but is perhaps their biggest service. It's estimated that nearly 850 million people use it. The thing about it, however, is many people don't even know they're using it.

What exactly is it? If you are familiar with Google Drive, then the concept is something you probably already understand. It's an online storage locker. But it's more than that. It is a place where you can store files, and it also syncs everything—so if you send a message on your iPhone, it appears on your MacBook and iPad. If you work on a Keynote presentation from your iPad, you can continue where you left off on your iPhone.

What's even better about iCloud is it's affordable. New devices get 5GB for free. From there the price range is as follows (note that these prices may change after printing):

- 50GB: $0.99
- 200GB: $2.99
- 2TB: $9.99

These prices are for everyone in your family. So, if you have five people on your plan, then each person doesn't need their own storage plan. This also means purchases are saved—if one family member buys a book or movie, everyone can access it.

iCloud has become even more powerful as our photo library grows. Photos used to be relatively small, but as cameras have advanced, the size goes up. Most photos on your Mac are several MB big. iCloud means you can keep the newest ones on your phone and put the older ones in the Cloud. It also means you don't have to worry about paying for the phone with the biggest hard drive—in fact, even if you have the biggest hard drive, there's a chance it won't fit all of your photos.

Where Is iCloud?

If you look at your MacBook, you won't see an iCloud app. That's because there isn't an iCloud app. To see iCloud, point your computer browser to iCloud.com.

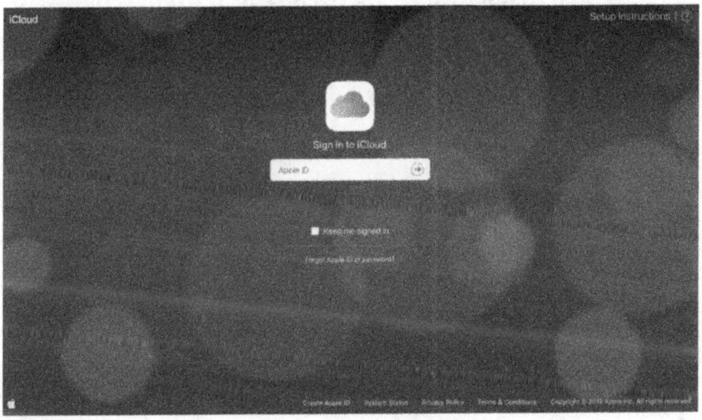

Once you sign in, you'll see all the things stored in your Cloud—photos, contacts, notes, files; these are all things you can access across all of your devices.

In addition, you can use iCloud from any computer (even PCs); this is especially helpful if you need to use Find My Mac, which locates not only your computer, but all of your Apple devices—phones, watches, even AirPods.

Backing Up Your Computer With iCloud

The first thing you should know about iCloud is how to back up your computer with it. This is what you will need to do if you are moving from one Mac to another.

If there's no iCloud app on the computer, then how do you do that? While there is no native app in the traditional sense that you are used to, there are several iCloud settings in System Preferences.

Open the System Preferences; at the top you will see your name and profile picture; click that. That brings up the option to manage iCloud.

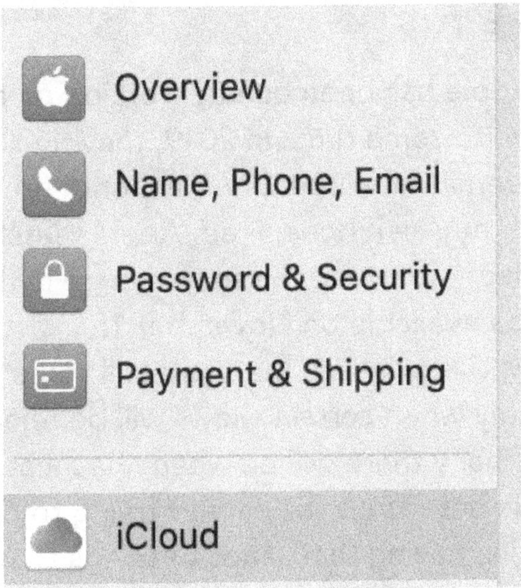

iCloud Drive

To see your cloud files, open the Finder app; on the left menu, there is an option for the iCloud Drive.

You can use iCloud Drive to create and move folders just like you would in the Finder app.

Apple TV+

Apple has been quietly working on a TV service for quite some time. In 2019, they finally revealed the details. It will be $4.99 a month (free for a year if you buy an iPhone, iPad, Apple Watch, Apple TV, or Mac—note that this may change in the future). It will be available on November 1.

At this printing, there are still some unknowns—notably when certain shows will be released and how many there will be when it launches. What Apple has said is they aren't trying to be like Netflix, having thousands of things to watch. They are focused on quality over quantity.

The shows that are planned to be released on November 1 (again, this could change after this printing):

- The Morning Show – A show about the drama behind the scenes of a morning TV show; it stars Jennifer Aniston, Reese Witherspoon, and Steve Carell.
- Dickinson – A period piece (with a modern flair) about the poet Emily Dickinson starring Haley Steinfeld.
- For All Mankind – An alternative reality drama that imagines what would have happened if the space race had never ended.
- See – An apocalyptic drama starring Jason Momoa about humans trying to survive in a world where nobody can see.

- The Elephant Queen – A documentary about the threat of elephant extinction.
- Snoopy In Space – A new series from Peanuts (i.e. Charlie Brown and company).
- Helpsters – A kids series from the creators of Sesame Street.
- Ghostwriter – A new twist to a 90s kids TV show.

More shows may be out in November, and more shows will definitely come each month—Apple plans to have at least one show / movie out a month. Apple has announced (with no set release dates) that it plans to work with such directors as J. J. Abrams, Steven Spielberg, and M. Night Shyamalan, and actors like Octavia Spencer, Brie Larson, and Jennifer Garner. A new Oprah Winfrey show will also be released.

You'll be able to, of course, watch these shows on Apple TV, iPhones, Macs and iPads.

Apple Music

Apple Music is Apple's music streaming service.

The question most people wonder is which is better: Spotify or Apple Music? On paper it's hard to tell. They both have the same number of songs, and they both cost the same ($9.99 a month, $5 for students, $14.99 for families).

There really is no clear winner. It all comes down to preference. Spotify has some good features—such as an ad-supported free plan.

One of the standout features of Apple Music is iTunes Match. If you are like me and have a large collection of audio files on your computer, then you'll love iTunes Match. Apple puts those files in the Cloud, and you can stream them on any of your devices. This feature is also available if you don't have Apple Music for $25 a year.

Apple Music also plays well with Apple devices; so, if you are an Apple house (i.e. everything you own, from smart speakers to TV media boxes, has the Apple logo), then Apple Music is probably the best one for you.

Apple is compatible with other smart speakers, but it's built to shine on its own devices.

I won't cover Spotify here, but my advice is to try them both (they both have free trials) and see which interface you prefer.

Apple Music Crash Course

Before going over where things are in Apple Music, it's worth noting that Apple Music can now be accessed from your web browser (in beta form) here: http://beta.music.apple.com.

It's also worth noting that I have a little girl and don't get to listen to a lot of "adult" music, so the examples here are going to show a lot of kid's music!

The main navigation on Apple Music is on the side menu:

- For You
- Browse
- Radio

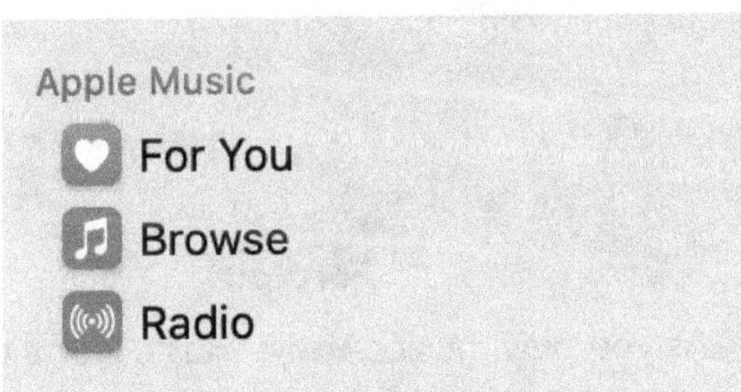

There's also a Library below this of what you have downloaded.

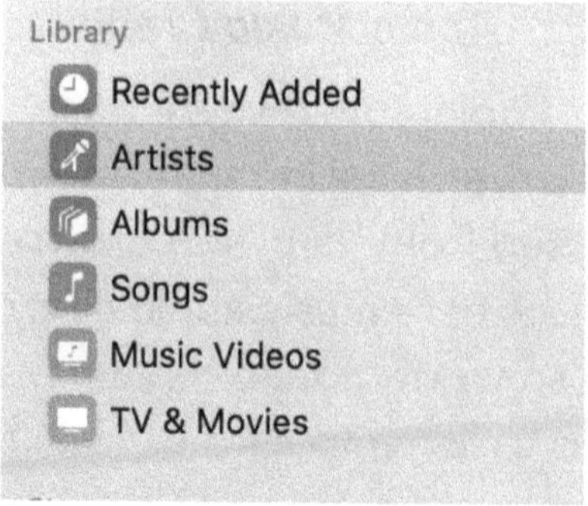

Library

When you create playlists or download songs or albums, this is where you will go to find them.

You can change the categories that show up in this first list by tapping on Edit, then checking off the categories you want. Make sure to hit Done to save your changes.

For You

As you play music, Apple Music starts to get to know you more and more; it makes recommendations based on what you are playing.

In For You, you can get a mix of all these songs and see other recommendations.

In addition to different styles of music, it also has friends' recommendations so you can discover new music based on what your friends are listening to.

Browse

Not digging those recommendations? You can also browse genres in the Browse menu. In addition to different genre categories, you can see what music is new and what music is popular.

Radio

Radio is Apple's version of AM/FM; the main radio station is Beats One. There are on-air DJs and everything you'd expect from a radio station.

While Beats One is Apple's flagship station, it's not its only station. You can scroll down and tap on Radio Stations under More to explore and see several other stations based on music styles (i.e. country, alternative, rock, etc.). Under this menu, you'll also find a handful of talk stations covering news and sports. Don't expect to find the opinionated talk radio you may listen to on regular radio—it's pretty controversy-free.

Search

The last option is the search menu, which is pretty self-explanatory. Type in what you want to find (i.e. artist, album, genre, etc.).

Listening to Music and Creating a Playlist

You can access the music you are currently listening to from the top of your screen.

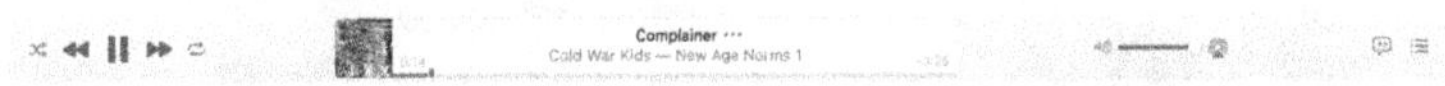

Right-clicking (two-finger clicking) on the album on this brings up several options. One is to take you to the album, which shows a full screen view.

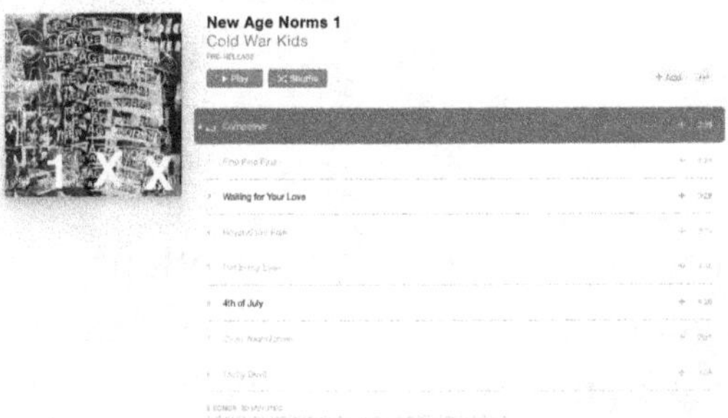

Clicking on the chat-like button will show you the text from what's playing.

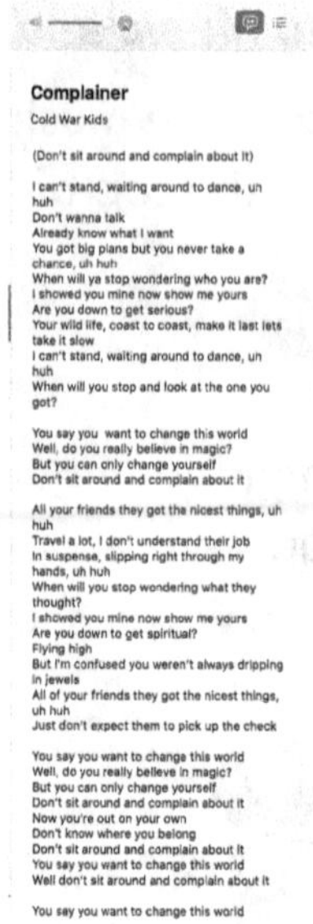

To the left of that is the option to select where you want to play the music. For example, if you have a HomePod and you want to listen wirelessly to the music from that device, you can change it here.

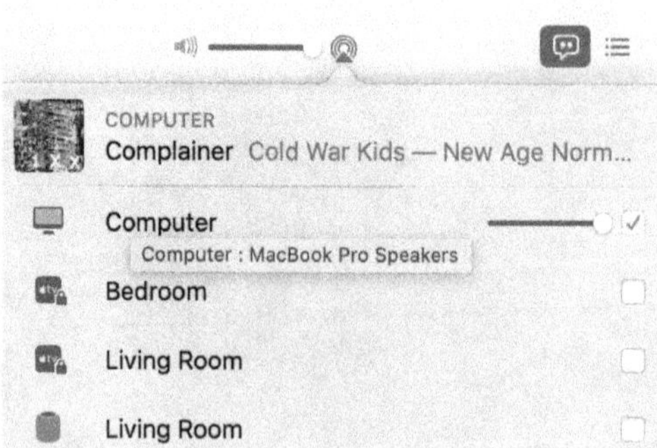

The option on the far right shows the next song(s) in the playlist.

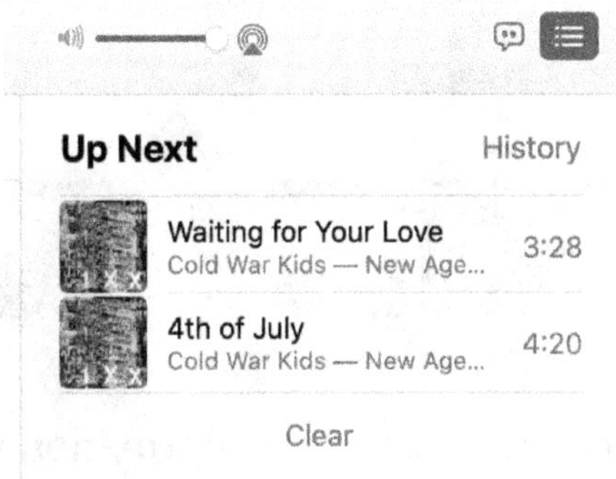

If you want to add a song to a playlist, then right-click the song and select the playlist (or create one).

At any point, you can tap the artist's name to see all of their music.

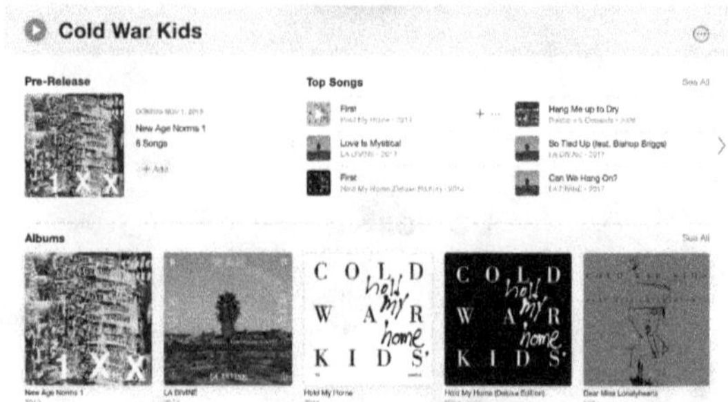

In addition to seeing information about the band, their popular songs, and their albums, you can get a playlist of their essential songs or a playlist of bands that they have influenced.

If you scroll to the bottom, you can also see Similar Artists, which is a great way to discover new bands that are like the ones you are currently listening to.

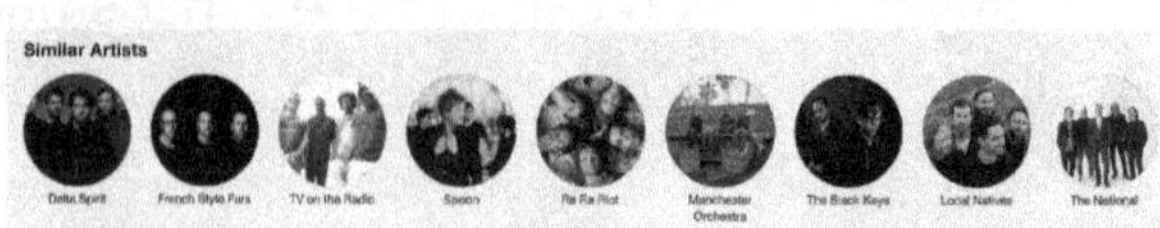

Tips for Getting the Most Out of Apple Music

Heart It

Like what you're hearing? Heart it! Hate it? Dislike it. Apple gets to know you by what you listen to, but it improves the accuracy when you tell it what you think of a song you are really into…or really hate.

Download Music

If you don't want to rely on wi-fi when you are on the go, make sure and tap the cloud on your music to download the music locally to your phone. If you don't see a cloud, add it to your library by tapping the plus, which should change it to a cloud.

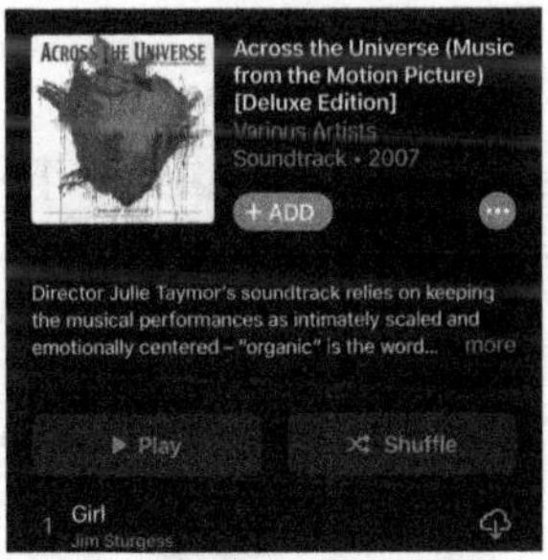

Hey Siri

Siri knows music! Say "Hey Siri" and say what you want to listen to, and the AI will get to work.

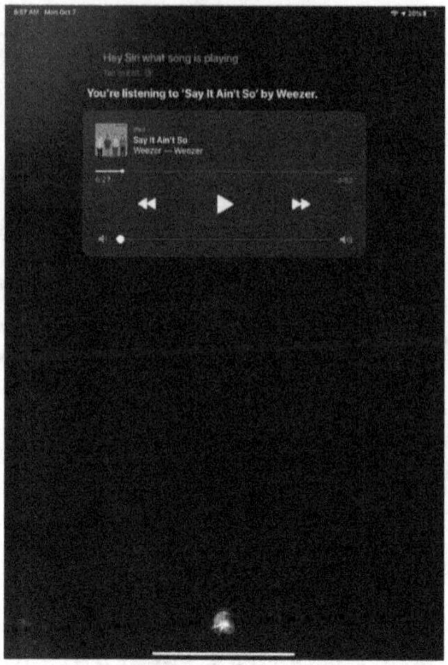

Apple News

In 2012, a little app with big ambitions called Next (it was later changed to Texture) disrupted the magazine industry by creating the Netflix of magazines. For one low price, you could read hundreds of magazines (and their back issues, too). They weren't small indie magazines—they were the big ones: People, Time, Wired, and more.

Apple took notice, and, in 2018, they acquired the company. The writing was on the wall: Apple wanted to get into print services.

In 2019, it was announced that Texture would close because Apple would release a new service called News+. News+ does everything that Texture did, but also combines newspapers (Los Angeles Times and The Wall Street Journal).

There is a free version of the service that curates news for you; the paid version that carries the magazine subscriptions is $9.99. (You can have five family members on your plan.)

What really makes Apple News stand out is it's curated for you and your tastes. If you have other family members on your plan, it will be curated for them as well—it's based on the user's tastes, so if you have a family member into entertainment news and you are into game news, you won't see their interests—only yours.

Apple News Crash Course

To get started, open the News app from your Launchpad.

The UI for the app is pretty simple—and is almost identical on iPhone and iPad, so there's limited to no learning curve if you already use it on one of those.

Today—This is where you'll find your curated news.

News+—Where you'll find magazines.

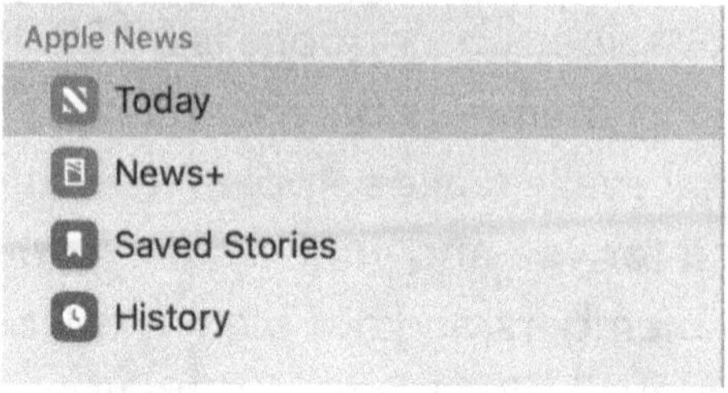

Today

The Today menu gives you all your news (starting with the top news / breaking news) in a scrolling format.

Right-click on any story and get several options.

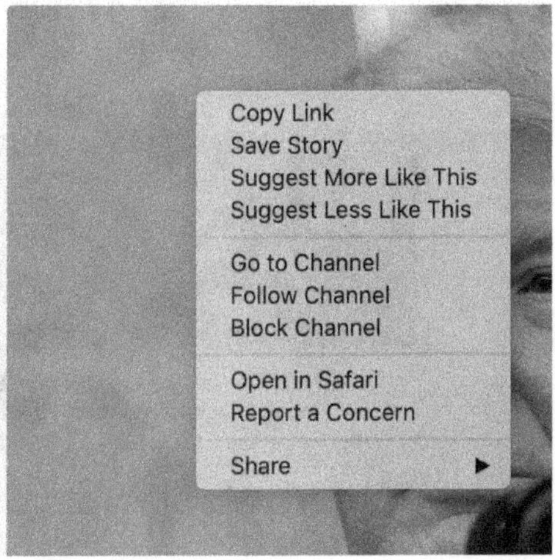

The one you will probably use the most is to suggest more / less like this; these two options help Apple News understand what you are into and will over time start to personalize stories based on your preferences.

Typically, "report" in a news app means you find it somehow inappropriate in nature; that's true here, but there are other reasons to report it—such as, it's dated wrong, it's in the wrong category, it's a broken link, or something else.

As you scroll down, you start seeing different categories (Trending Stories in the example below); when you tap the three dots with a circle, you'll get an option to block it, so it won't show in your feed any longer.

When you tap to read a story, there are only a few options.

To make the text larger or smaller, use the view option in the menu above and zoom in or out.

One criticism of Apple News by some has been its UI; when Apple announced the service along with its partnership with the Los Angeles Times and Wall Street Journal, many expected a format similar to what you have seen with the magazines section—a full newspaper-type layout.

Worse, many didn't even know how to find the newspaper. And if they did find it, they couldn't search for stories. While the app is pretty resourceful, this is still an early product and some of the features you want might not be there yet.

That said, you can "kind of" read the Los Angeles Times (or any newspaper in Apple News) in a more traditional way. First, find an article in your feed from the publication you want to see more from, and then click the publication's name at the top of the story.

This will bring up the publication along with all the topics from that publication.

If you want to search for a particular story or publication, then use the search box in the upper right corner.

News+

The last section to cover is News+; this is where you'll find all the magazines you love.

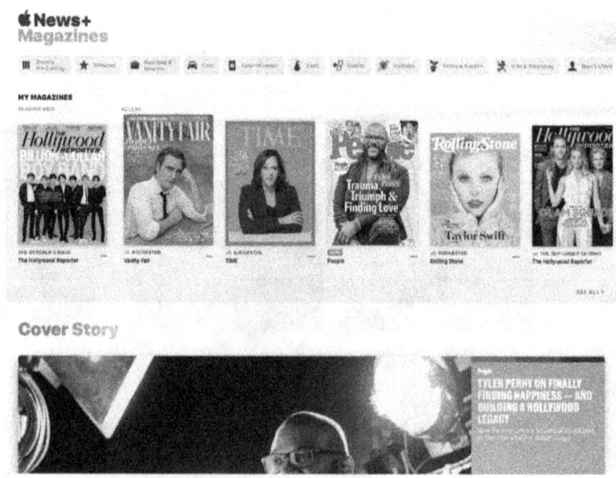

The format is similar to the Today screen; magazines you read are at the top; below that are stories pulled from several different magazines that the app thinks you'll be interested in.

When you read articles from the list, it opens in the actual magazine and looks a little different from articles in the Today area.

Anytime you want to read more from a magazine (or see back issues) just click the logo from an article you are reading.

That brings up a list of all the issues you can read as well as some of the latest stories from the magazine.

Right-clicking on the magazine cover brings up several options—including the option to Follow the channel, which lets you know when new issues are available.

To browse all the magazines available, select Browse the Catalog from the main screen (or browse by a category that you are interested in).

This brings up a list of all the magazines you can read (at this writing, there are around 300).

[8]

I Know How It Works, Show Me How to Dress It Up!

This chapter will cover:

- System preferences
- Adding social networking and other accounts
- Controlling sound
- User groups
- Screenshots
- Photo continuity
- Accessibility
- Privacy / security

So now you know the basics; you should be able to work your way around the desktop with ease and use all the basic programs comfortably. But it still doesn't feel quite...you. It still has all the default settings, colors, gestures, and backgrounds. Sure it's a cool computer, but now let's make it feel like your computer.

System Preferences

All of the main settings are accessed in System Preferences which is essentially the Mac equivalent of Control Panel on a Windows computer. So to get started, let's get to System Preferences by clicking Launchpad, then clicking the System Preferences icon.

You can also get there by clicking on the Apple in the upper left corner of the menu and clicking System Preferences.

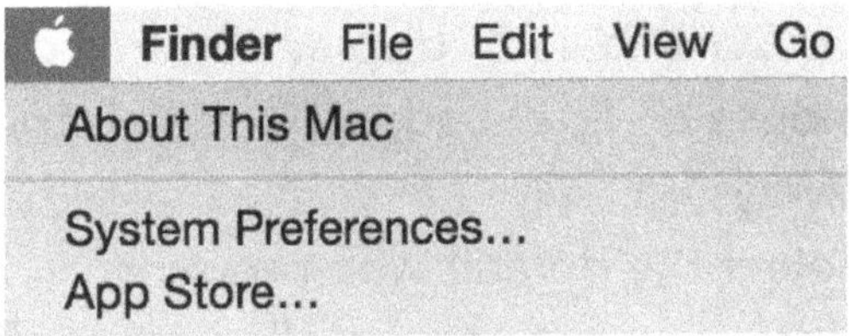

Once the app opens, you'll see there are lots of things that you can configure.

General

Let's get started with the first option: General. Under General, you can:

- Change the appearance of the main buttons, windows, and menus by selecting either Blue or Graphite.
- Choose the highlight color.
- Change the top menu bar and Dock to dark colors. This option works well with dark wallpapers.

- Set scroll bars to display automatically based on mouse or Trackpad, only when scrolling, or always on.
- Select the default web browser.
- Here is where you can allow Handoff to work between your Mac and iCloud devices (some older Macs don't support this feature).

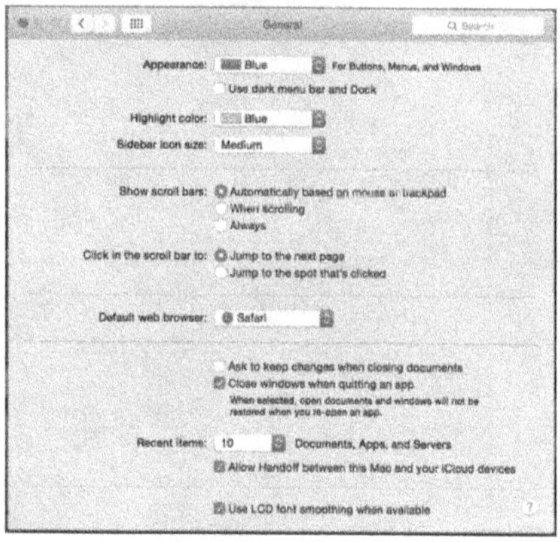

At any time, you can get back to the main System Preferences page by clicking on the button with 12 tiny squares. You can also hit the Back button, but if you are several menus in, you may have to hit the Back button several times.

Desktop & Screen Saver

The Desktop & Screen Saver section will help you change perhaps the most visually noticeable thing on your Mac—the desktop wallpaper. Along the left sidebar you will see several different dropdown options: Apple, iPhoto, and Folders.

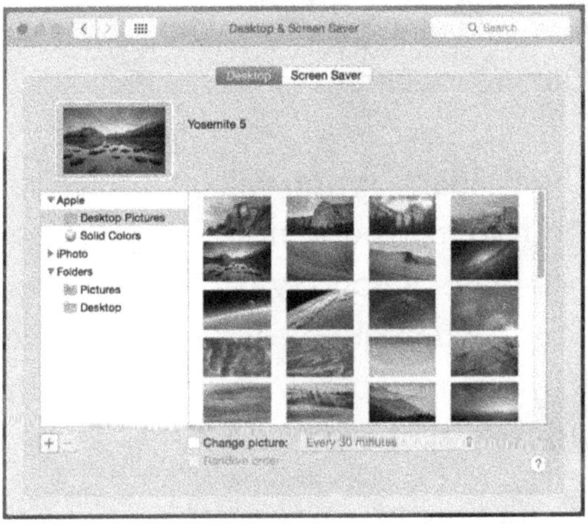

At the bottom, you will be able to change the picture every so often, and you can choose how often you'd like a new image to refresh. The images that show up in the right-hand window will be the ones that get scrolled through during refreshes.

To change your desktop wallpaper to one of the great-looking images provided by Apple, or if you just want to browse the available choices, click on the Apple name. A bunch of colorful, high-resolution images will populate the right-hand side, and you can scroll through the list to find something you like. Clicking on an image will change your wallpaper to that particular selection. If you're a plain Jane and prefer to keep things really simple, you can also select Solid Colors to find an array of potentially yawn-inducing plain wallpapers.

Selecting iPhoto will let you scroll through your photos, allowing you to select a cherished memory as your wallpaper.

The Folders option will let you choose between added folders where more image files might be lying in wait. If you save lots of images to your desktop, you might want to add the Desktop folder here so you can include those images as would-be wallpapers.

Adding and Removing Folders

1. To add new folders and image collections, click on the '+' button located at the bottom of the left sidebar.
2. When the window comes up, search for the folder that you'd like to add.
3. Once you find the desired folder, click the blue Choose button to confirm the changes.
4. To remove a folder, highlight the folder that you'd like deleted and then click the '–' button to remove it.

Screen Saver

To set one up, click on the Screen Saver button at the top of the Desktop & Screen Saver window.

The left sidebar will have more options than you probably need when it comes to different ways to display your pictures. Some great ones you will probably like are Shuffling Tiles, Vintage Prints, and Classic.

On the right side you can see a preview of what your screen saver will look like. In this part of the window you can also select a source: National Geographic, Aerial, Cosmos, Nature Patterns, and Choose Folder if you have a particular folder of images you'd like to use. If you'd like to shuffle the order in which images appear, check the box next to Shuffle slide order.

At the very bottom of the window you can choose the length of time before the screen saver starts. You'll also be able to pick if you'd like to display the clock or not.

Dock

There isn't a lot you can do to the Dock and most of these settings are self-explanatory. For the most part the settings just make things a little more...animated. Magnification, for example, makes an app icon larger when you hover your mouse over it.

One option I will point out, however, is the option to automatically hide and show Dock; all of these settings are a matter of taste; I personally choose to hide the Dock for two reasons: one, it gives you more screen space, and two, it lets you use the Dock while you are in a full screen app.

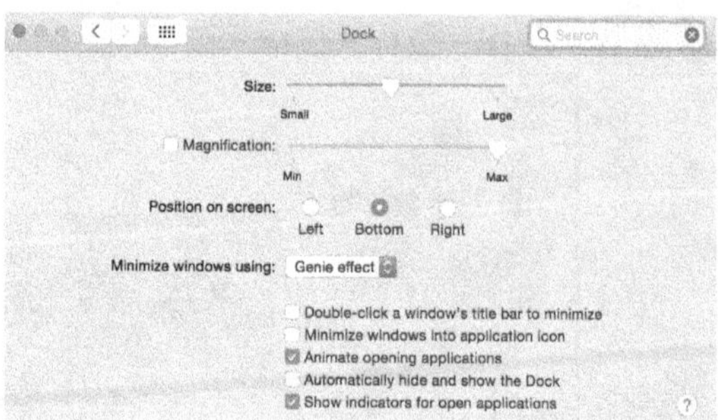

Mission Control

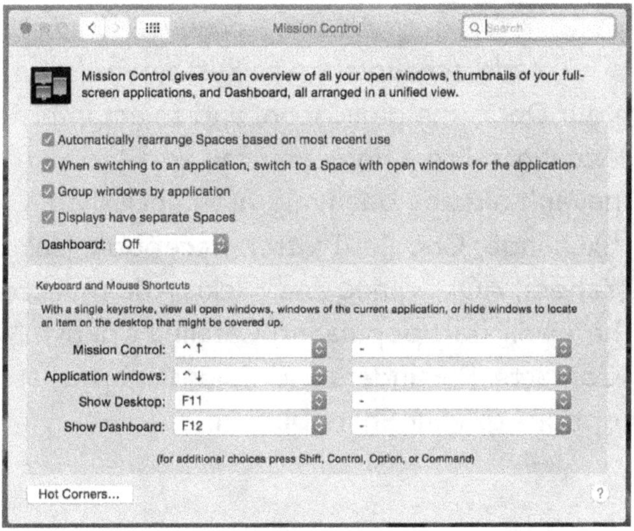

Mission Control is where you can set different parts of your screen to do different things. What do I mean by that? For example, you can set up a shortcut so that every time you move your mouse to the far upper right corner, your desktop is revealed. You can also set up shortcut keys on your keyboard. Mission Control is really about helping you make simple tasks quick.

Social Networking, Mail, Contacts and Calendars

When you use Twitter, Facebook and other apps, you may be used to just going to a website. On a Mac, you can add them into your computer's information, so you don't need to login; this also lets you get notification pop ups when you have new messages, likes, etc.

Adding Accounts

To add accounts, go to System Preferences on your Dock (the gears icon) and select Internet Accounts. From here, you can add accounts that haven't already been migrated, including iCloud, Exchange, Google, Twitter, Facebook, LinkedIn, Yahoo!, AOL, Vimeo and Flickr. Adding accounts here will start populating Catalina's native Mail, Contacts, Reminders and Calendar apps, and add options to your Share button.

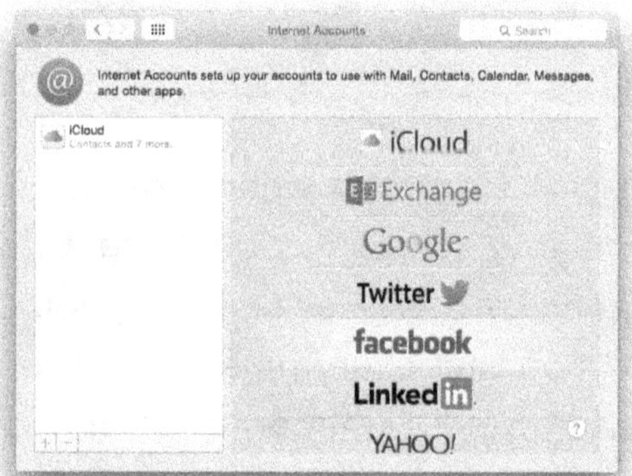

Note: You can also add accounts within the Mail, Contacts, Calendars, and Reminders apps by opening each app and clicking File > Add Account.

Twitter, Facebook, LinkedIn, Vimeo and Flickr

Catalina OS supports deep Twitter, Facebook, LinkedIn, Flickr and Vimeo integration. To get started, simply sign in to your account(s) from System Preferences > Internet Accounts. Select Twitter, Facebook, LinkedIn, Flickr, or Vimeo, and then enter your username and password. From now on, you'll be able to use that account with the Share button throughout Catalina and receive notifications in your Notifications Center.

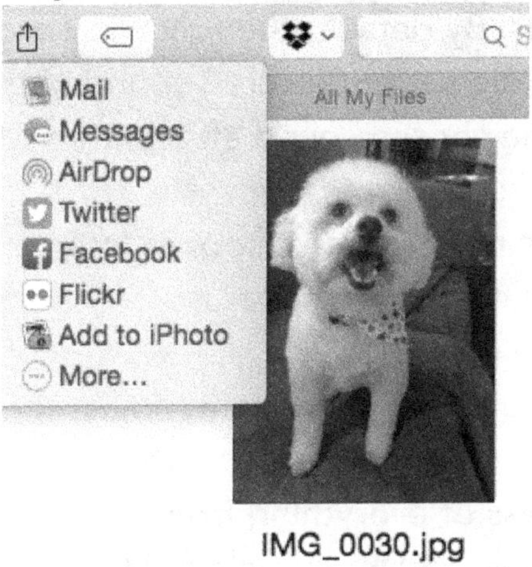

SOUND

As the name implies, the Sound menu is where all changes related to sound effects and sound in general can be modified. There are three tabs that you can switch between.

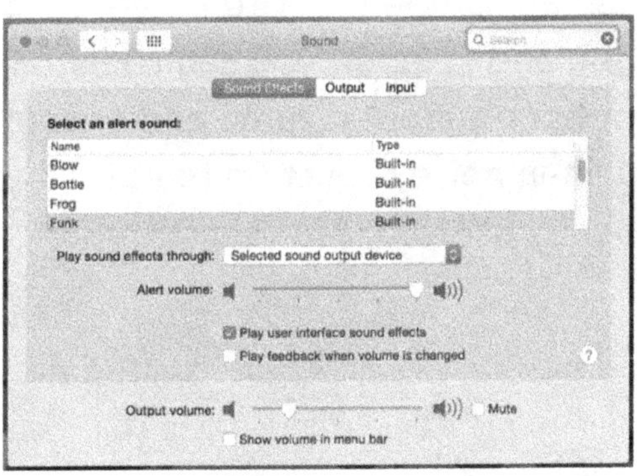

Sound Effects

The Sound Effects tab is where you can select an alert sound from the many different built-in options. By default, the following dropdown menu should be set to Selected sound output device to play the chosen sound effects through your standard speakers.

The next two checkboxes let you turn sound effects on or off for the user interface, and for volume control.

Lastly, you'll be able to adjust the output volume of your speakers. This will affect the loudness of everything from sound effects to music that's currently being played through the computer.

Input & Output

The input and output tabs are both very similar. Each will let you change the device for sound input or output (speakers or microphones), as well as adjust sound settings. In the output tab, you can adjust the slider to move the balance left or right, and in input, you can change the microphone's input volume and enable or disable the built-in noise reduction feature in case you frequently use your Mac's microphone in busy cafes.

Users & Groups

If your Mac is for family use and a couple of people will be using it, then this setting will come in handy.

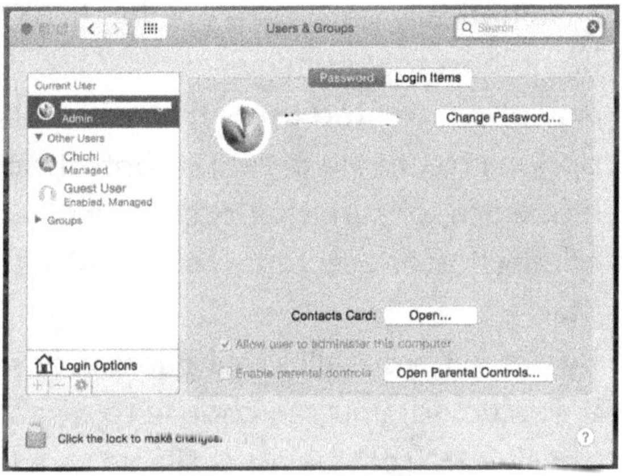

Along the left sidebar all existing users and groups (if you have any) will be laid out for you. To make a change to an existing user, first you need to choose the "Click the lock" icon and unlock it; unlocking lets you change settings to the user. You will also be asked for your password at this time—this is all a safety measure to ensure that if you accidentally left your computer unattended, someone couldn't come along and lock you out of your own machine.

Below are a few things you'll be able to do with each user. Depending on the type of user it is (admin, guest, child, etc.), some of the settings won't be available.

- Selecting the admin user account will let you change the login password, open up the Contacts card and enable parental controls. Clicking the Login Items will allow you to change the applications that start running automatically each time you log in. There has to be at least one admin user.
- Any other created users that you make will have options to enable parental controls, change password, or turn that account into another administrator account that has full control of the Mac.
- By default, you will see a guest user set up. If it's selected, you can choose to disable the guest user from being available as a login option. You can also set parental controls and allow guest access to your shared folders. If you do choose to keep the guest user, keep in mind that there will be no password required, and all information and files created during that session will be deleted upon logging out.
- At the bottom of the left sidebar there is another option, called Login Options. This is where you'll find different options such as automatic login, show password hints, and show the Sleep, Shut Down, and Restart buttons. You can also display your full name or user name at the top right of the menu bar by checking the box next to Show fast user switching menu and making a selection.

Create New Users

So you know how to manage the primary user, but what about creating additional users? That's pretty simple. Just follow these steps (and make sure you have already hit that lock button to unlock the option).

1. Click on the '+' button.
2. From the New Account dropdown menu, choose from the following options: Administrator, Standard, Managed with Parental Controls, or Sharing Only.

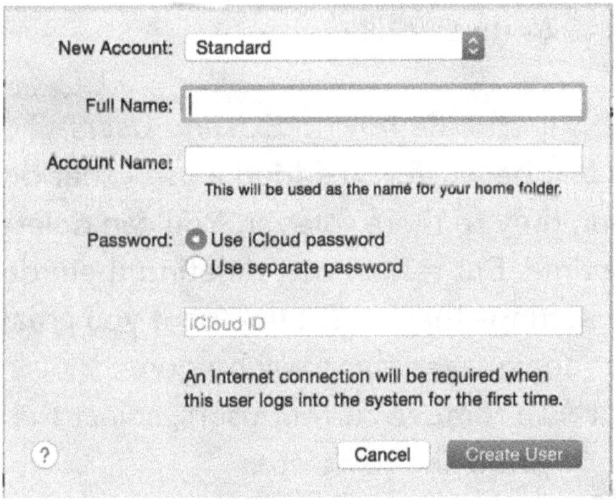

3. Fill in the Full Name and Account Name fields. These don't have to be real names. Mickey Mouse can have a user name if you want.

4. You can choose to have the new user log in using an existing iCloud account and password, or create a whole new password.

5. If you selected Use iCloud Password, you will be prompted to enter the associated iCloud ID.
6. If you instead choose to opt for a newly-created password, you will be asked to enter it twice to verify it.
7. Once finished, click the blue Create User button. If you chose to use an iCloud ID, you will be asked to enter the password. If you made a new password, you don't need to do anything else.

Removing Existing Users

Just because you added a user, that doesn't mean they're there forever. You can delete them at any time. But remember, deleting them deletes all the settings they've set up—so if you create that user again, everything will be gone.

1. To remove current users, select the user that you'd like to delete.
2. With that user highlighted, click on the '–' button.
3. A prompt will appear asking if you are really sure you'd like to remove the user from the computer.

4. You can also choose from one of three radio buttons: save the home folder, leave the home folder alone, or delete the home folder.
5. Once you've made a decision, click the blue Delete User button to confirm your choice and make the changes happen.

Creating Groups

If the computer is being used in a place where there are dozens of users (a classroom or library, perhaps), then creating a group would be a good option for you.

1. At the bottom of the left sidebar, click the '+' button.
2. From the New dropdown menu, select Group
3. In the Full Name field, create and enter a name for your group.
4. Click the blue Create Group button to confirm.
5. The new group will be created, and you will be able to check boxes next to each existing user to designate who will be a part of this group. If you have existing groups, you can also select entire groups to be a part of yet another group.

Snap This

Screenshots on MacOS have always been pretty simple and straightforward. Shift-Command-3 to take a screenshot of your entire screen and Shift-Command-4 to take a screenshot of a specific area of your screen.

These commands still work, but Apple took it up a notch and allows you to edit the screenshot—if you've taken screenshots on iOS, then the experience is probably familiar to you.

As soon as you take a screenshot, you'll see options for what you can do next in a small popup at the bottom right of your screen. These options will take you to a Markup window where you can add annotations, shapes, text, and more.

In addition to these options, MacOS has added a new command: Shift-Command-5. This opens up a screenshot interface with several options such as capture entire screen, selected window, or a selected portion. The last two options are new: record the entire screen or record a portion of it.

Continue That Photo Where You Left Off

One thing Apple has done really well with their devices is continuity—the idea of stopping on one device and picking up where you left off on another. For example, you could stop a movie in the living room on Apple TV and continue watching it on your Apple TV in the bedroom. Or you could get a text on your Apple Watch and reply on your phone. It's all very intuitive and just works.

This concept of using on one device and picking up on another now extends to the camera. With OS Catalina, you can take a picture on your iPhone or iPad and have it automatically sent to your Mac and into the photo editing app of your desire.

If the Mac app supports the feature, then you'll see it under Edit in the menu area; there will be a new option that says "Insert from Your iPhone or iPad" with the option to Take Photo or Scan Documents.

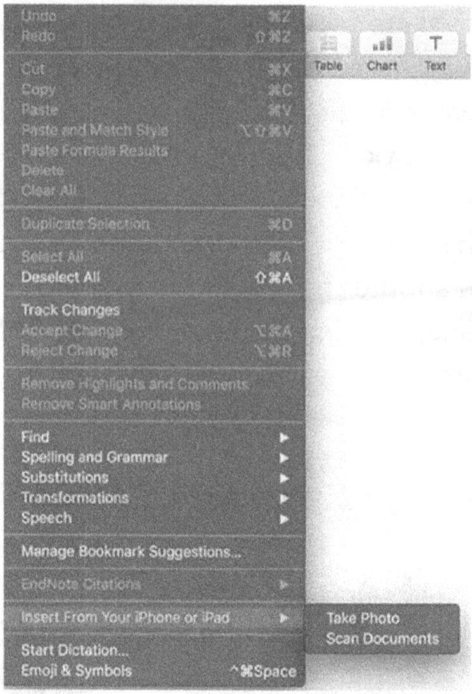

Once you snap the photo on your phone or tablet, it will automatically appear in the document.

Parental Controls

If kids are using your computer, then Apple has Parental Controls to help you make sure the kids don't get into trouble. It's a pretty powerful app, but it does have a few limits—if you want ultimate protection, then there are also several paid apps like NetNanny (www.netnanny.com). Parental Controls is also good for guests—if you don't mind if people use your computer, but you only want them to use the Internet and have no access to anything else, then you could set it up like that.

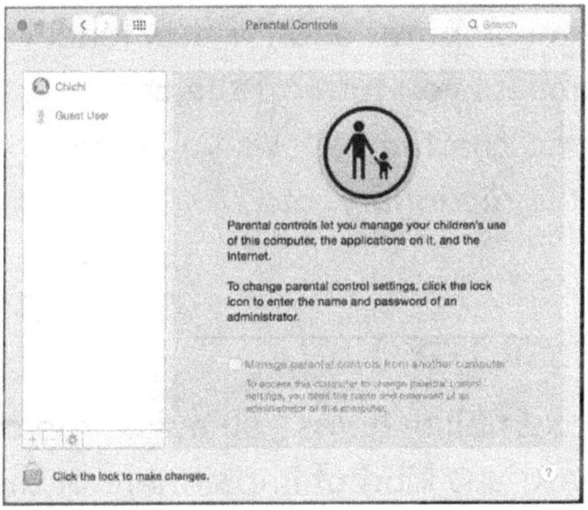

To use Apple's Parental Controls, first make sure you have created a user account for your child. Next go to System Preferences and Parental Controls.

If the padlock on the lower left corner is locked, then click it to unlock it and type in your password.

You can now set up parental controls for each child user. You can make it as restrictive as you want. The first tab lets you pick what apps they can use. You could block all apps except games, for instance. The next tab lets you control web usage. By default, Apple will try to filter out adult content. If this is a young child, then a better option might be picking the web pages they can access—you could, for instance, block every Internet website except Disney. The next tab is People. This lets you select who they can email and message—you could limit them to only emailing parents and grandparents, for instance. The second to last tab lets you pick time limits. You can pick when they use the computer and for how long. And finally, the last tab lets you turn off the camera so they can't do video chatting, allows you to hide profanity from the dictionary, etc.

ACCESSIBILITY

Accessibility helps you adjust the computer if you have any kind of impairment or disability. It lets you change things like making the display larger, having a voiceover that describes what's on your screen, and put captions on videos when available.

To open Accessibility, click System Settings and Accessibility. On the left side of the box that comes up will be all the various things you can change. Clicking on each one will create more options.

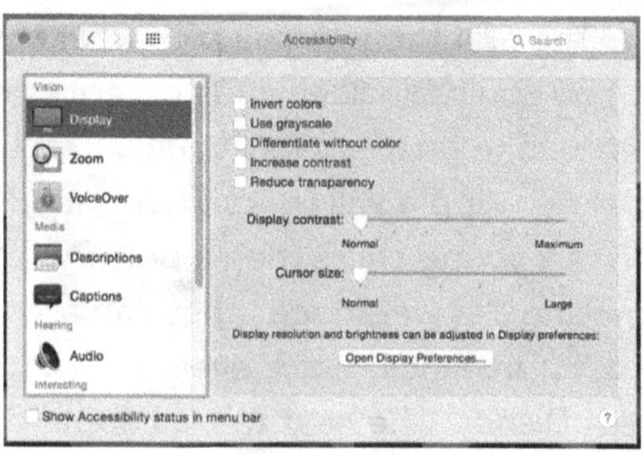

Vision

Under Display, you can make the screen grayscale, invert colors, decrease the contrast, etc. Zoom allows you to create a zoom effect over smaller areas of the screen when you hit a keyboard shortcut. VoiceOver reads back any text that's on the screen.

Media

The Media section includes a few different settings for audio and video playback. Click on Descriptions to enable spoken descriptions for videos.

Captions will apply subtitles and captions to videos.

Hearing

The Sound tab provides options for the hearing disabled. You can choose to set up a visual flash of the screen each time an alert sound is played, and also decide if you'd like to play stereo audio as mono instead.

Interacting

Keyboard includes settings for Sticky Keys and Slow Keys. Sticky Keys allows certain buttons to remain activated without you having to hold down the key. For example, if you have Sticky Keys turned on and want to copy some text, instead of holding down Command-C at the same time, you could press the Command button first, followed by the C key. When enabled, you'll hear a lock sound, and any time you use a modifier key like Command, a large icon will appear in the top right corner of the screen indicating that a Sticky Key combination has been started. Slow Keys increases the amount of time between a button press and activation, so if you press Enter, it will take a little longer to actually process.

Mouse & Trackpad features settings like Mouse Keys, which lets you move the mouse around using the number pad on your keyboard, double-click speed, and the option to ignore the built-in Trackpad (on MacBooks) if there is a separate mouse or Trackpad connected to the computer.

Switch Control requires you to enter your administrator password before making any changes, because it's a powerful function that allows you to control the computer using one or more switches that you designate. You can also modify other settings like what to do while navigating, determine pointer precision, and change the size for the Switch Control cursor.

The Dictation tab does exactly what it sounds like—it lets you dictate commands and write or edit text using only your voice. To enable dictation, you first need to click on the bottom button that says Open Dictation & Speech Preferences and selecting the On radio button.

VOICE CONTROL

Voice Control lets you control your computer with your voice.

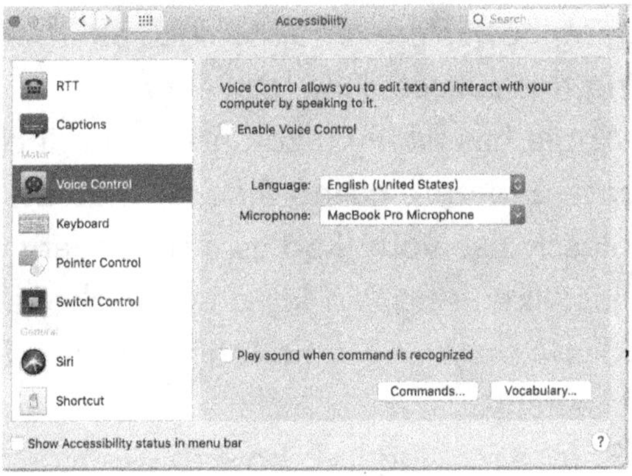

SIDECAR

What's Sidecar? It's basically using your iPad as a second screen alongside your Mac.

Using your iPad as a second Mac screen is nothing new. Popular apps such as Duet have been doing this successfully for years.

Apple has finally taken note and decided to release a feature called Sidecar that lets you wirelessly use your iPad as a secondary Mac screen; it's just like using AirPlay on your phone to show YouTube on your TV. So long apps like Duet, right? Not exactly.

Before moving into how to use Sidecar, let me first mention what Sidecar is not: a rich app full of pro features. It does one thing very well: shows your Mac screen on your iPad. Apps like Duet are compatible with iPhone and iPad and also work with cross OSes—so you can also show your Windows device on your iPad. But personally, one thing I find lacking on Sidecar is touch. I expected to be able to tap the iPad screen and launch apps and folders. That wasn't the case. It was for display purposes only...unless you have an Apple Pencil. Sidecar feels like it was made to entice people to buy an Apple Pencil. With an Apple Pencil, touch suddenly becomes possible. There's probably a good reason for this—the Apple Pencil is more precise and has more gestures than your finger.

So now that you know a little about what it isn't, let's look at how it works.

First, make sure your MacBook (yes, this is only compatible with MacBooks—sorry Windows users) is up-to-date with the latest OS (Catalina).

Second, make sure your iPad is turned on, in standby mode, and on the same Wi-Fi network (if not, you won't see the next step).

Third, go to the menu in the upper right side of your MacBook and click the rectangular box for AirPlay.

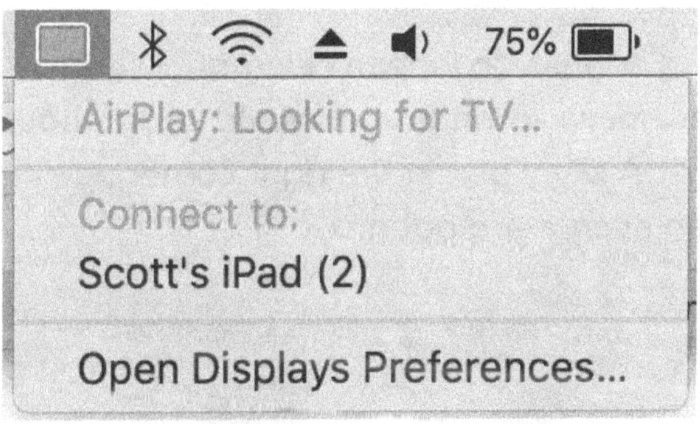

That's it! Kind of. Your MacBook should now be showing on your iPad. It will look a little like this:

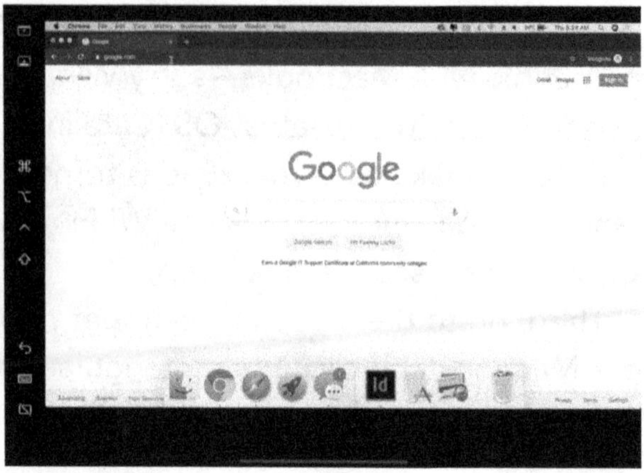

So what do I mean "kind of"? There are still a few more settings you should know about. Click that AirPlay box in the right corner again and you'll see even more options.

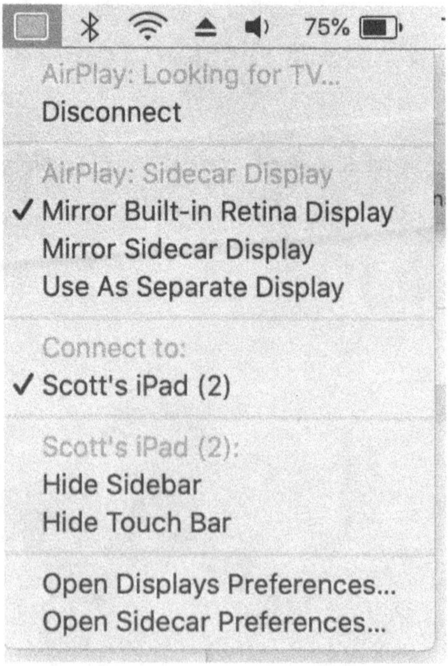

What are all these options? Use As Separate Display (vs the two Mirror options) turns your iPad into a second screen—so you can have another Mac app running on your display instead of just showing whatever is on your MacBook. The two Hide options get rid of the boxes you see on your iPad to make it a bit more full screen.

Finally, Open Sidecar Preferences will give you a few additional options. You can, for example, pick to show the menu bar on the right instead of left.

You can disconnect from Sidecar by either tapping on the box with the line through it on your iPad or going to the AirPlay button on your Mac and disconnecting.

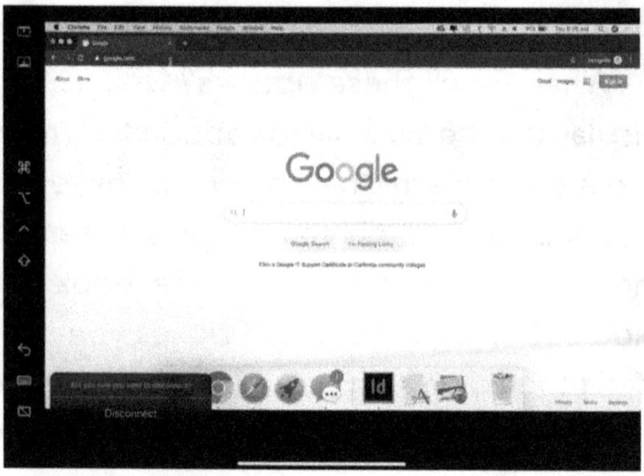

Privacy and Security

If your computer is in a place where other people can get to it, or if you are just generally concerned about your privacy being violated, then head on over to Privacy and Security in the System Preferences.

Creating Strong Passwords

Strong passwords are the first line of defense against potential hackers (or smart children!); a strong password is not something like "password"; a strong password has letters, numbers and even symbols in it. It could be something like this: "@mY_MACb00k."

You can use the Password Assistant to test how strong your password is.

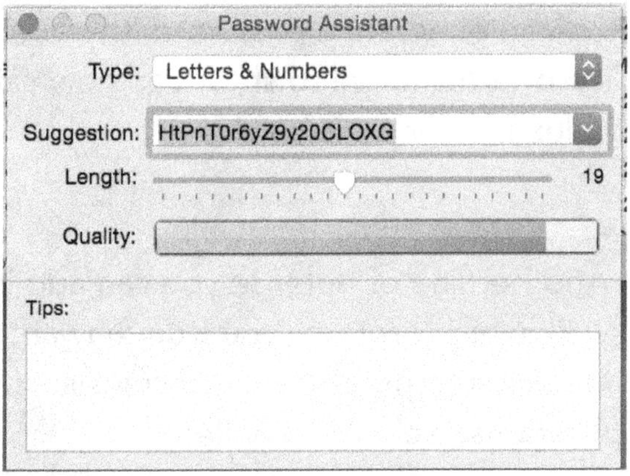

When Keychain loads, you will be able to view the entire list of accounts that are already synced to Keychain. If you would like to change the password for an account that already exists, find the account and double-click on it. If not, click on the '+' button at the bottom to add a new account.

When the new window comes up, take a look at the bottom. There will be a field for password, and at the right of it will be a small key icon. Click the key icon to open up Password Assistant.

From Type you can select Manual (create your own), Memorable, Letters & Numbers, Numbers Only, Random, and FIPS-181 compliant.

Suggestions will automatically populate, and you can scroll through several different suggestions by using the dropdown menu.

Adjust the length slider to make the password longer or shorter. Any password you create will meet at least these requirements to be considered fair.

As you generate a password, the quality indicator will change to show you how safe and complex a given password is.

Firewall

Another line of defense you can add is a firewall, which protects you from unwanted connections to potentially malicious software applications, websites, or files.

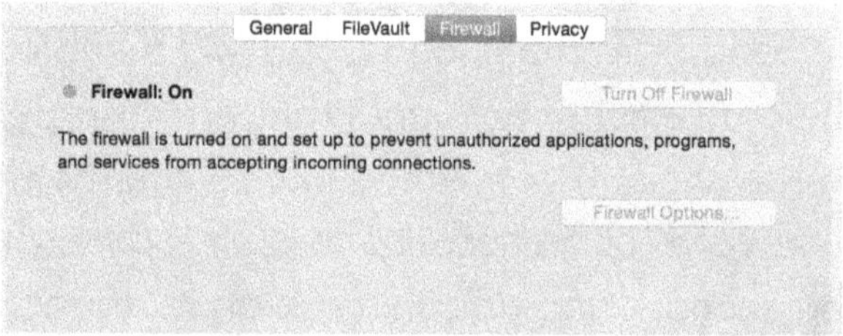

To enable the firewall that comes with your Mac, go to System Preferences > Security & Privacy and select the Firewall tab. Before you can make any changes, click on the lock icon in the bottom left corner and enter your administrator password to continue.

Find My Mac

Just like your iPhone or iPad, Mac comes with a handy feature called "Find My Mac" which lets you find your computer if someone steals it or you just misplace it; you can also wipe its hard drive clean remotely.

To enable Find My Mac, go to System Preferences > iCloud and check the box next to Find My Mac. Your location services must also be turned on, so go to System Preferences > Security & Privacy > Privacy > Location Services and make sure Enable Location Services is checked on.

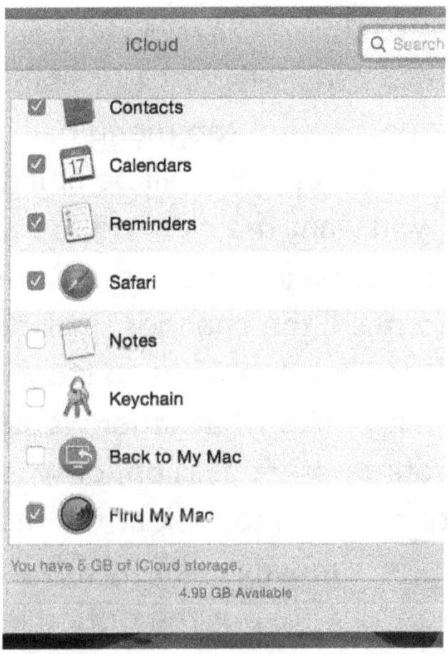

To track your computer, you can log into any computer and visit iCloud.com, enter your iCloud login information, and click on Find My Mac. As long as the Mac is awake and connected to the Internet through Wi-Fi or Ethernet, you will be able to play a loud sound, lock it, or completely erase it so your private information is removed.

Privacy

Apple knows people worry about privacy; they have lots built in to help you control what can (and can't) be seen.

Internet Privacy

If you'd like to clear your search and browsing history, there are two ways to do it: either by clicking on Safari > Clear History and Website Data or History > Clear History and Website Data. Both can be found on the top menu bar. When the window comes up, you will be able to choose how far back you want the clearing to reach. Once you make a selection just press the Clear History button to make the changes final.

Cookies allow websites to store data and track certain things, like what other websites you visit during your Internet session, or what kind of products you tend to look at the most. This information is mostly used by advertisers to better target ads for you, but the option is always there if you'd like to disable them. Open up Safari, go to Safari > Preferences, then select the Privacy tab. The cookie options range from allowing all websites to store cookies to blocking all websites. You can also allow cookies only from the most frequently visited websites. If you prefer not to be tracked, check off the box at the bottom that says Ask Websites To Not Track Me. Some websites will not function as you may want them to by disabling this feature.

Application Privacy

The other part of privacy is through installed applications. Go to System Preferences > Security & Privacy and click the Privacy tab. You can shut Location Services off by checking the box next to Enable Location Services. Browse through the left sidebar and you'll be able to customize permissions. If you don't want any apps to access your contacts or calendars, here is where you can block some or all programs from that information.

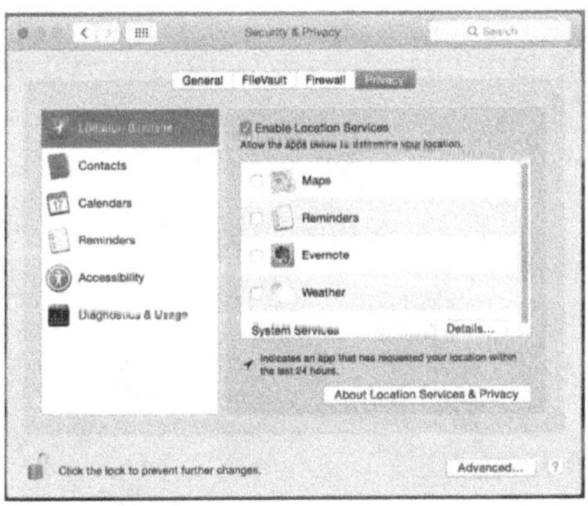

Screen Time

Screen Time might be something you are familiar with. It's been on iPads and iPhones for a while. It comes to MacOS with the Catalina update. What is it? It's a productivity setting that lets you restrict how long you can use certain apps (games for instance). It's highly customizable, so you can set one app like Word to have zero restrictions, but another one like Internet to have limits.

Screen Time isn't an app in the traditional sense; it's an app within your system settings. To use it, go to System Preferences, then click Screen Time.

This launches a new window that tells you how much time you've been on your computer.

You can set up a passcode by clicking on options at the bottom of the window.

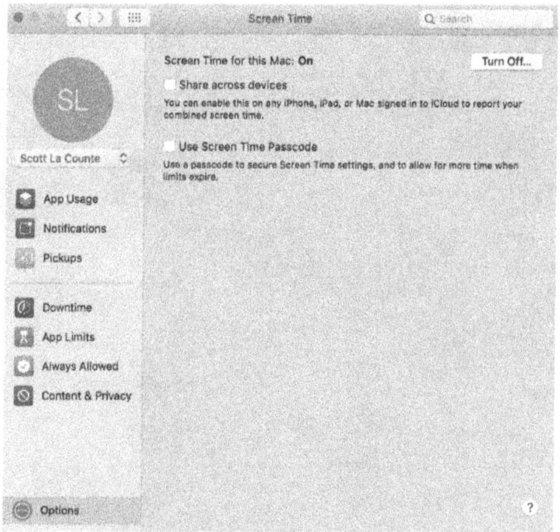

App Limits is where you can start restricting certain apps. Click the '+' in this section.

From here select the app (or kinds of apps) that you want to limit.

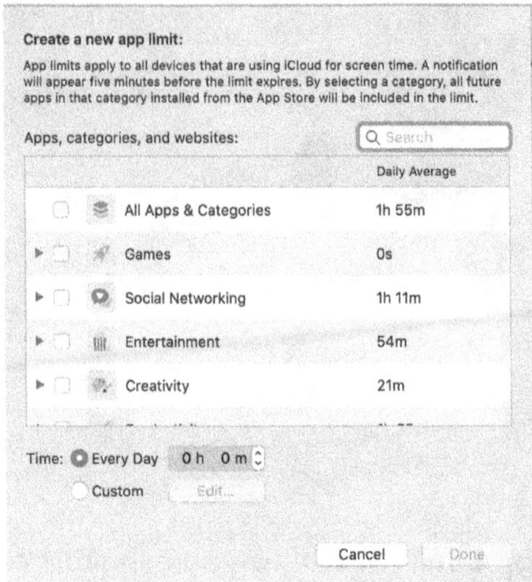

At the bottom, you can say how much time you want to set the limit to.

Under Always Allow, you can select apps that have no restrictions.

Screen Time
Search
SL
Scott La Counte
App Usage
Notifications
Pickups
Downtime
App Limits
Always Allowed
Always allowed apps are available during downtime, or if you selected the "All Apps & Categories" app limit.
Allowed Apps:
Search
Sort by Daily Usage
Daily Usage
Microsoft Word
3h 27m
Messages
3h 27m
App Store
3h 22m
Google Chrome
3h 22m
Music
3h 7m
Mail
1h 20m
Sketch
45m

[9] Keep It Running Smoothly

This chapter will cover:

- Preserving battery life
- iCloud
- Time Machine
- Software updates

Macs feel more like an investment than other computers; with that in mind, you obviously want to protect and maintain your investment. In this chapter, I'll cover how.

Preserving Battery Life

If you are using an iMac, then this section will obviously not apply since iMacs don't run on battery, but if you have a MacBook, then this section is for you.

Most MacBooks can easily get over six hours of battery life, but there are things you can do to get even more.

- Go to System Preferences > Energy Saver and under the Battery tab, choose to put hard disks to sleep whenever possible, and dim the display slightly while on battery power. You don't want to set it too low, or you'll find it going to sleep when you are reading or doing a task that doesn't require movement.
- Keep the screen only as bright as you need to clearly see the screen. The F1 key will minimize the brightness and F2 will make it bright again. If you are at the beach then you will want the brightest, of course; but if you are in a dark room do you really need full brightness? Probably not.
- The keyboard also has brightness that can be adjusted with F5 and F6 on your keyboard. Backlight on the keyboard really helps in a lowlight setting, but when it's broad daylight, you really don't need it—even at the brightest, you probably would not even be able to tell that it's on.

- When you run websites with Flash, you are killing your battery. Be cautious of what you are using—especially if you are low on battery.

iCloud

iCloud lets you store things like photos and videos online. It's kind of like Google Drive or Dropbox. Best of all you get 5GB for free. Lots of cloud-based storage sites give you more storage than Apple—so why use it?

- You'll be able to back up your contacts so they are synced perfectly across your Mac, iPhone, iPad, and iPod. Make a change in a contact card or add a new contact, and the change or addition will be reflected across all of your synced iCloud devices.
- Media files purchased through the iTunes Store won't count against your storage.
- It makes files available across all of your Mac devices.

If you haven't set up an iCloud account, you can create one by going to System Preferences > iCloud and following the on-screen instructions. Once you're finished, you'll be able to select what kind of data you'd like synced through iCloud: Photos, Mail, Contacts, Calendars, Safari, Notes, Keychain, and more. At the bottom you will notice a bar that indicates how much storage has been used up, and how much available storage you have left.

If you want more storage, you can pay extra. The following are the rates as of this writing:

- 20 GB for $0.99 a month
- 200 GB for $3.99 a month
- 500 GB for $9.99 a month
- 1 TB for $19.99 a month

If you decide to change your mind and don't need the extra storage plans, Apple gives you 15 days to contact them and ask for a refund.

Time Machine

Everyone worries about losing their data; Apple helps you out with one of their most powerful behind-the-scenes apps: Time Machine.

Time Machine will back up all of your files, applications, and settings with minimal configuration or headache. In the case of a catastrophic event such as hard drive failure, having a Time Machine backup can allow you to quickly recover all of your data and applications, and even all of your settings (such as your desktop background and even the specific location of icons on your desktop).

You will need to buy an external USB or Thunderbolt hard drive. It is recommended to buy a drive that is larger than the current used space on your computer. For example, if you have used 100 gigabytes of space on your computer's hard drive, you should buy at least a 120-gigabyte hard drive.

You can also purchase an additional Time Machine Airport Capsule that does all of this wirelessly.

To get started, plug the hard drive into your computer and Time Machine will start automatically. It will ask you if you would like to use the drive as a Time Machine Backup Disk. Choose Use as Backup Disk.

If Time Machine does not start automatically, go to Finder > Applications > Machine, and click Choose Backup Disk. Select your new hard drive.

After you specify the drive to use as a backup, Time Machine will automatically begin backing up your data.

Software Updates

If you want your computer running smoothly then make sure you update regularly; updates are free and come once every couple of months. They fix minor bugs and sometimes add things to correct vulnerabilities that might make your computer open to viruses.

MacOS X, by default, will prompt you when updates are available, and you need only to click "Update" and enter your password in order to run the updates. Sometimes, in the case of major updates, you will need to restart your computer to complete the update. You can click Not now if you would like to delay the updates until a more convenient time.

BONUS BOOK: HOW TO USE SAFARI

[1] WELCOME TO SAFARI

This chapter will cover:

- Using the toolbar
- Understanding tabs
- Private browsing
- Reader Mode
- Bookmarking

Just as a Windows computer has Internet Explorer as the default web browser, Mac has Safari as the default web browser; if you've used Safari on your iPhone or iPad then you should already be accustomed to it.

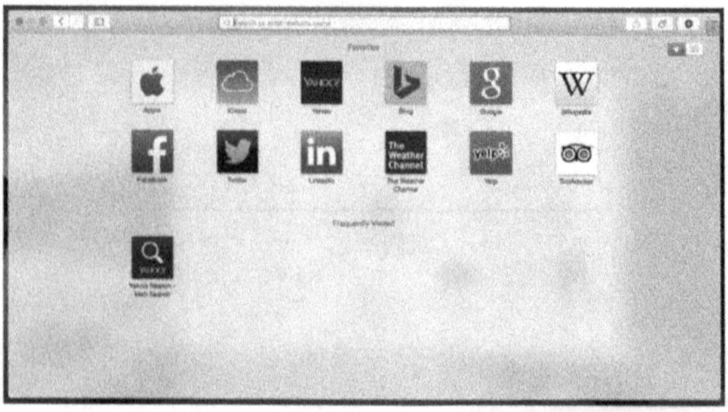

Noticeably absent from Safari is something called "Flash." Flash is what you might have used to watch some videos and other web apps; you can always download it, but this will affect the battery life if you're on a laptop, as Flash tends to drain the battery quickly—which is one of the reasons Apple does not include it. You can download it from Adobe if it's essential to your searching; just google "Flash for Safari browser" to get the free download.

One of the biggest advantages of using Safari over another web browser is a feature called Handoff. Let's say you're reading an article on your phone on the subway coming into work, and when you get to work and want to pick up where you left off on a larger Mac screen. Just open up Safari, then click the two square boxes in the upper right corner.

If your iPhone or iPad is synced with the computer, then you'll see its name and the pages that it's currently browsing. It's not the most obvious feature—you might miss it the first time you try it, but it's there. It's at the bottom; it will have a cloud with your device's name and then the webpage under it. Click the webpage name and it will launch the page.

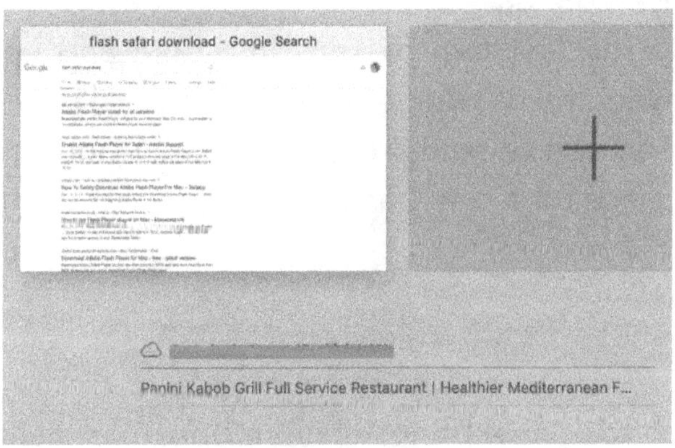

You can also handoff a Mac page to your iPhone or iPad in the same way.

In addition to websites, Handoff also lets you seamlessly sync things like Maps, Messages, and documents (Pages, Numbers, and Presentation documents).

SAFARI CRASH COURSE

The Toolbar

So now that you know about Handoff, how do you actually use Safari?

Let's start at the top—literally. Some of these features will probably be more obvious than others, but in the tradition of keeping it simple, I'll cover even the easy stuff.

The first two buttons (the right and left arrows) make the webpage go either forward or back to the previous or next webpage. The button next to this brings up a side panel.

The panel brings up your bookmarks and reading list (we will cover this in a little bit more detail shortly).

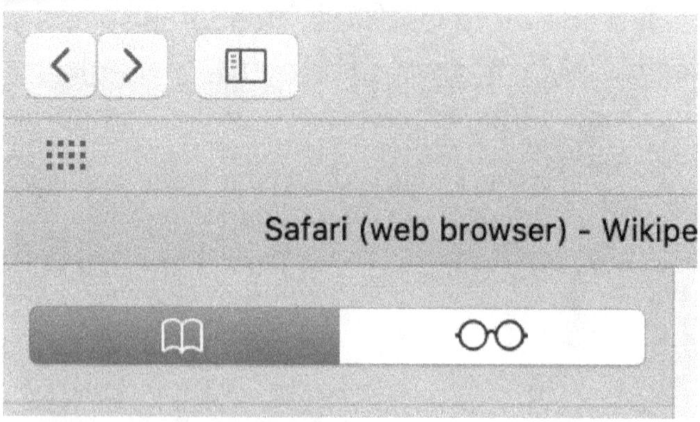

Right smack in the middle is the address bar, which doubles as a search bar. What does that mean? It means if you know the webpage you want to go to, you can type it in; but if you want to search for something, just type in the name and it will search for it in whatever search engine you've set up (Google, for example).

Over on the right side, you have your Download button (which won't be there if you haven't downloaded any files—or if you've cleared the files that you've downloaded).

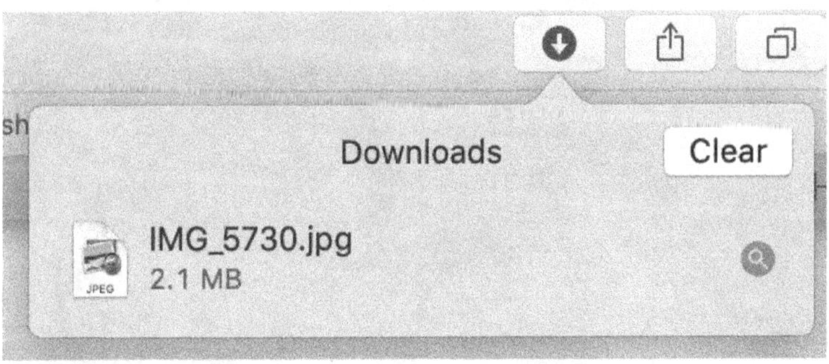

Next to Download is the Share button; you can click this button to email the webpage you are currently on. You can also use this button to bookmark a page or add it to your reading list.

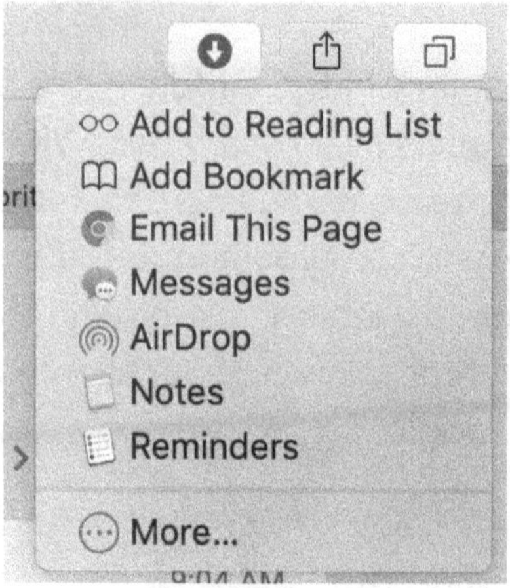

The "More..." option under Share will bring up a list of possible extensions (I'll cover extensions later in this book).

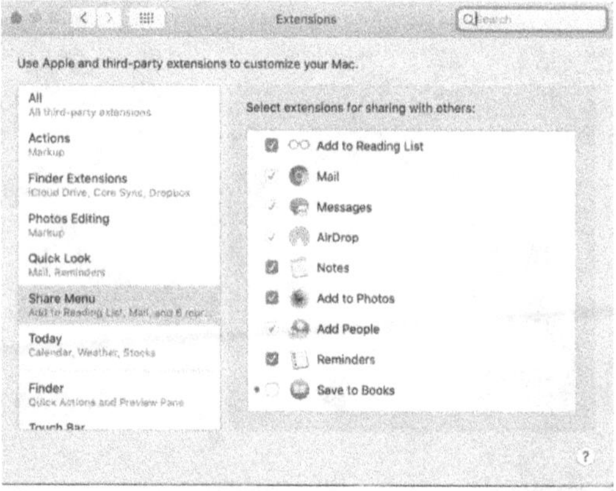

The top toolbar is a bit...bare; there might even be options on there that you don't want. If you right click (or click with two fingers) on your trackpad, you'll see an option that says Customize.

This brings up all kinds of things you can put in your toolbar. It also puts the toolbar into edit mode so you can drag stuff (or move stuff) off your toolbar that you don't want.

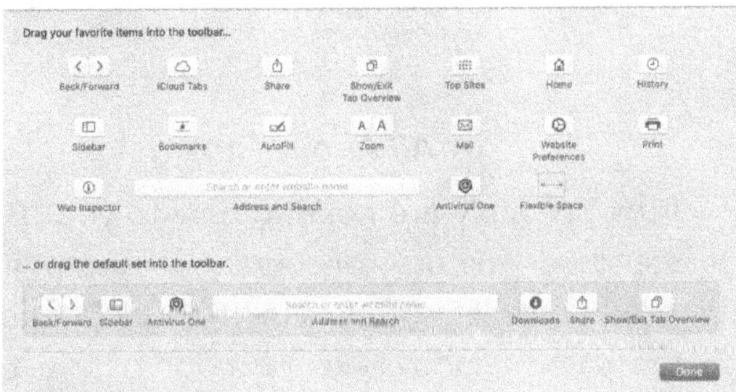

Once you click what you want on your toolbar, you can drag it to where you want it to go. If there's something on the toolbar that you don't want, just drag it down and let go.

All About Tabs

Tabs probably are nothing new to you. They are a standard feature on every popular Internet browser. Tabs let you have multiple webpages open in the same window—so you don't have to have several windows open. It helps keep everything nice and organized.

Below is an example of tab browsing.

Alternatively, below is an example of having them in windows instead.

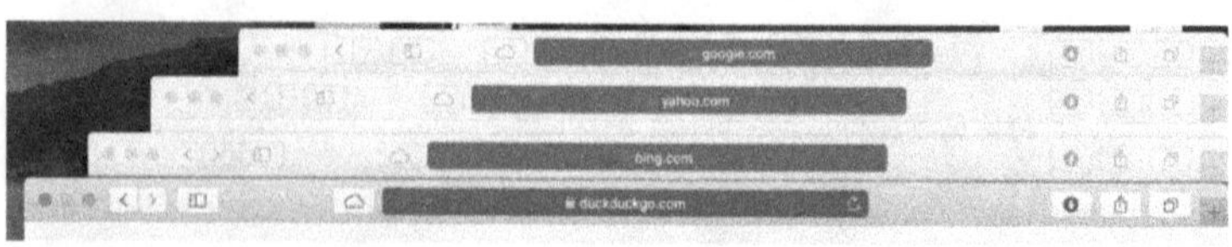

You can open a new tab by clicking on the plus button (+) to the right of the tab bar.

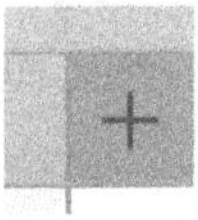

If you click and hold that button, you can also bring up a list of all your recently visited webpages.

Just like you could right click on the toolbar to see more options, you can also right click on the tab bar. The option I find most helpful is Close Other Tabs—this quickly closes all your opened tabs.

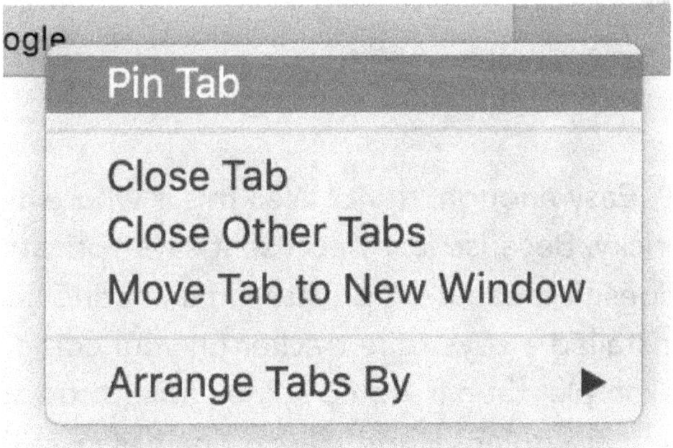

Private Window

If you go up to the top menu and click file, you'll see a little option called "New Private Window." It's a very useful (and misunderstood) feature, so let's talk about it.

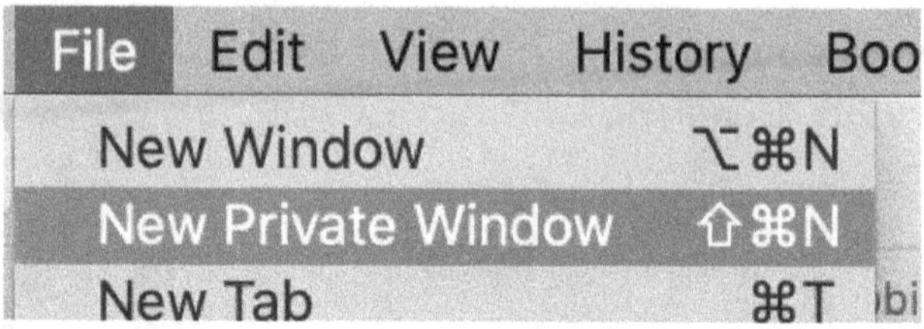

At its core, New Private Window is like an isolated Internet session where nothing is remembered. So if you type in "I love Smurfs" there's no record of it! It looks just like a normal browser window but it's a different shade and has a message about it being in private mode.

Easy enough, right? Well this is where it gets tricky. Because just because it says "private" that doesn't mean it is "private." If someone had installed a keystroke tracker on your computer, for example, then it would still be able to track what you are doing. Hopefully no one has installed a keystroke tracker on your computer though!

More importantly, however, is that just because the browser isn't keeping track of what you are doing doesn't mean your computer or server is also ignoring everything—those things are quite nosy! If you are on a work computer using private mode, for example, your employer could still monitor you. If you are on a home computer and you are downloading a file that is illegal, your IP will know what you are doing.

What's the lesson here? Don't do anything stupid (or illegal) because you think your session is private.

So why use private mode at all? Personally, I use it for things that I don't want cookies to track—for example, I want to shop on some website for my wife's birthday; I don't want my wife to sit at the computer and see that I was shopping on some site for her birthday! If I had to do banking on a public computer, then I'd also use this mode because it's safer than the other.

A History of You

Your browser keeps a pretty long record of what you are doing—unless you are in private mode. That can be both a blessing and a curse.

If you are ever on a public computer or just want to erase your history for whatever reason, then click Safari > Clear History.

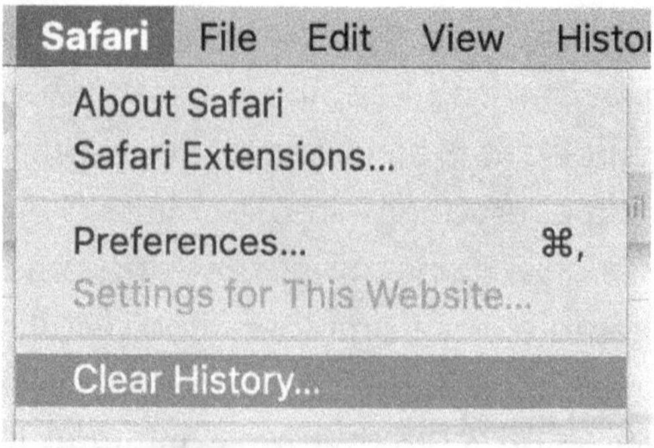

If you'd like to see what's actually in your history, then just click on History in your top menu.

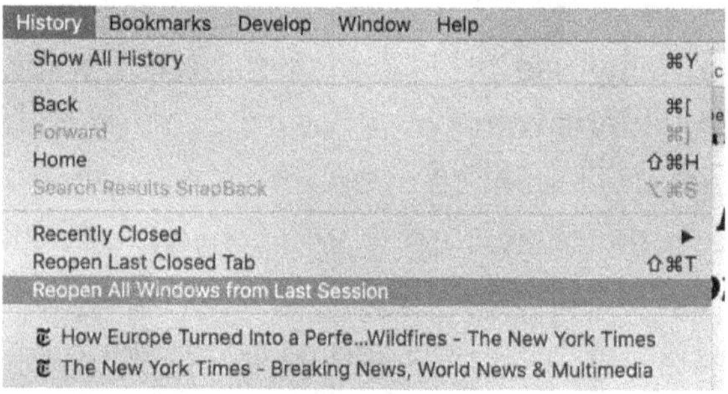

From History you'll see your recent history, but can also click Show All History. This is helpful for two reasons. One, you can see your history by date. So let's say you can't remember some article you read, but you know what date you read it on. You can drill down to that date and see everything you looked at.

Over on the right side, you can also search your history. So, for example, if you want to see everything you read from NYTimes.com, then you can search for that term and see everything.

Bookmarks / Reading List

I've quickly covered how to add webpages to your bookmarks and reading list. Let's look at it in more detail.

Reading List is the easiest, so let's start there. When you add something to your reading list, you are telling Safari you want to read it later. You can put anything here, but ideally, it's best suited for articles.

Once they're in your reading list, you can right click on any name to see a list of options; if you happen to be syncing with your phone, you can Save Offline to read it when you don't have data. You can also go here to remove an article.

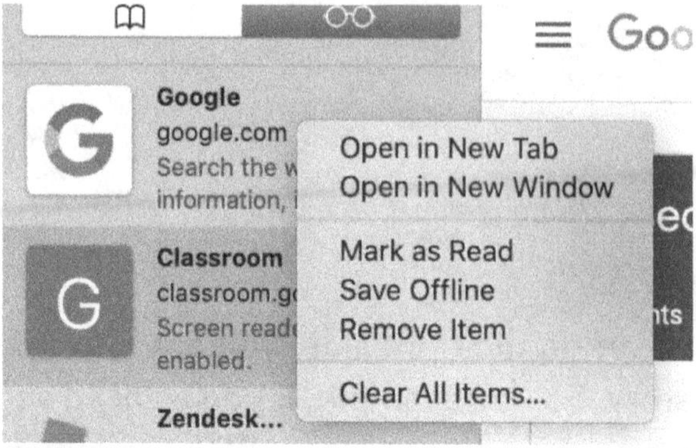

When you bookmark something, there are a few more options. You'll get a dialog box and the first option is Favorites.

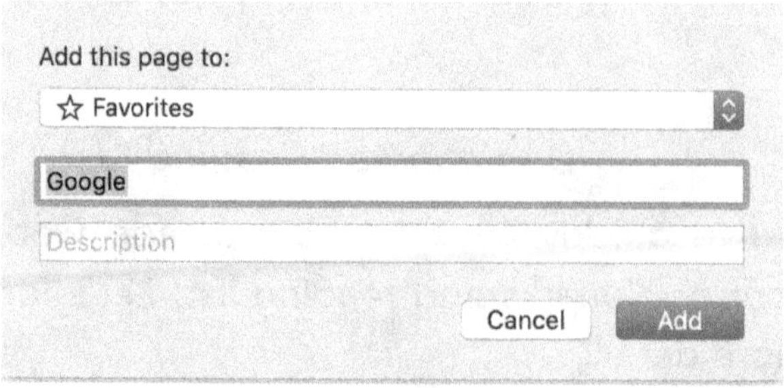

When you open a new tab, you'll see the Favorites right up on top. These are basically your go-to websites that you are always going to, so it's best to keep the list somewhat short; you can click any of those icons to move them around.

If you click the dropdown in the previously shown dialog box, then you'll see all the possible folders for your bookmarks (if you have any), or you can just stick it in the general bookmarks folder.

Once you open the bookmarks sidebar, you can right click on any entry to bring up options—including deleting or renaming the bookmark.

You can also create a bookmark folder here. Once you create a folder, you can immediately name it (or you can name it later by right clicking and bringing up the options menu).

Once you have a bookmark folder, you can drag any of your bookmarks into it to stay organized.

Exporting

The bad thing about the Internet is it's always changing; the article you read yesterday may not be there tomorrow. Printing is nice to have a record of something…if you like to waste paper and ink.

The better option is to export it as a PDF and then store it on your computer; this will work great for articles and standard web entries. If you try to do this with something with some sort of JavaScript (a report, for example), then you probably won't like the results.

To try it, go to File > Export as PDF.

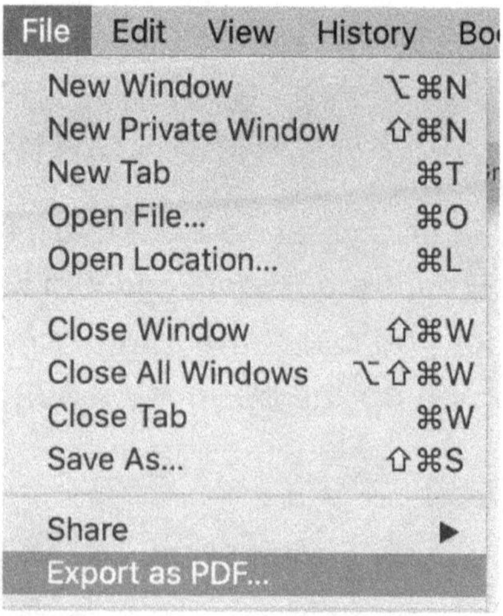

Reader Mode

A few years back, Safari released a nice feature called Reader Mode. As the name suggests, this gives you a more reader-friendly version of what you are reading online.

Here's an example of a normal article:

And here's that same article in Reader Mode:

The mode helps eliminate some of the common, flashy ad distractions you can see on websites. It works great for blogs and other online publications, but it's not for everything—you won't see this mode, for example, while you are shopping online.

If the mode is available, then you will see a little paragraph button in your top toolbar. Click it to enable this mode.

You can also access this view (when available) under View > Show Reader.

Emoji That

Chances are at some point you will want to send an email with an Emoji. Just whip on out the Emoji keyboard, right? Not exactly. This is possible on your mobile device, but it's a bit different on a desktop or laptop. It's still pretty easy, however.

When you are ready to add an Emoji, just go to Edit > Emoji & Symbols from your top menu.

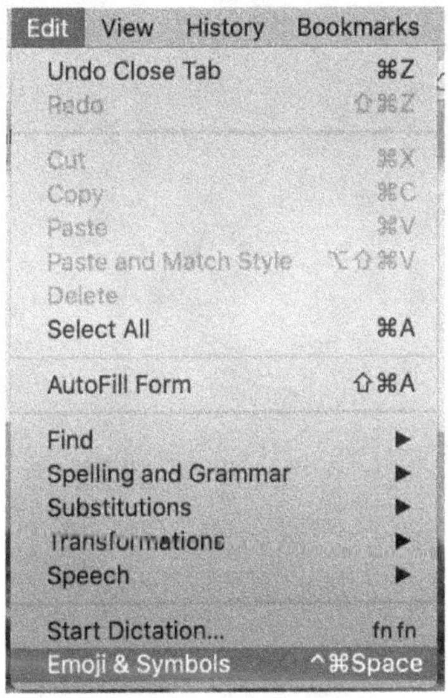

This will bring up a dialog box with all the possible Emoji's. Once you see the one you want, just click it.

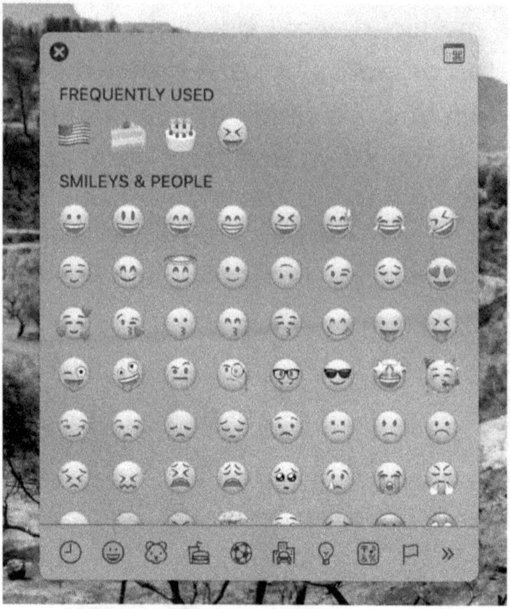

Find It

Have you ever searched for something on Google, then gone to the page and wondered where on earth it is in the result for that term? You can go to Edit > Find and search for the term to see where exactly the term comes up on the page; you can also hit Command F on your keyboard to do this.

Customize Your Start Page

When it comes to browsers, Safari has come a long way, but Chrome is still king and they've pioneered a lot of features that are now finding their way to Safari. One of these is just how personal you can make Chrome.

Apple has caught on and has brought customization of its own to Safari. It's called the Start Page. The idea is anytime you open a new tab (or your closed browser) this is the first thing you see. You can customize it to show the pages you visit most, what's on your browsing history on another device, and more. But perhaps the best feature is adding any photo you want.

To customize the page, open a new tab, then go to the control icon in the bottom right corner. Check off what you want to display on your Start Page.

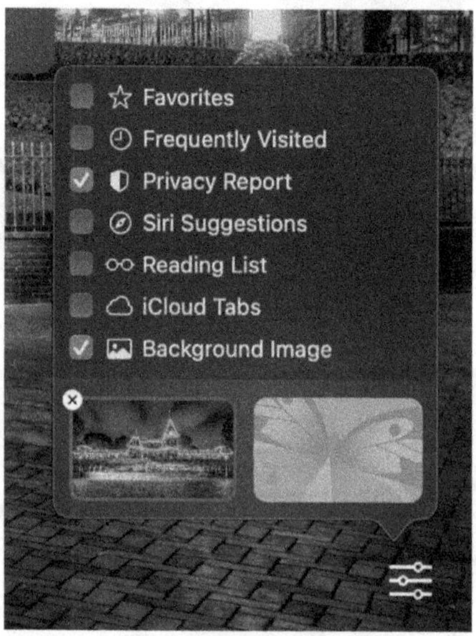

To add a photo, just click the + icon.

You can also add a photo by finding it on your computer, then dragging it into the Start Page.

What's Up Dock?

Down in your dock bar, there's a final list of options. Just click with two fingers on your trackpad while your finger is over the Safari icon.

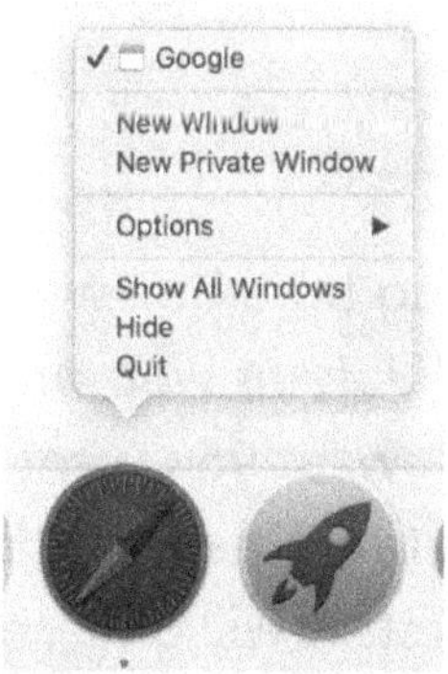

Default Browser

What if you want to use Safari, but you don't want it to be your default browser? That's an easy fix.

Go to the Launchpad, then select System Preferences.

Next, go to the icon that says General.

This will bring up a box with a few options; one of them says "Default web browser." Click that and select what browser you want. If you want Firefox or Chrome, but don't see it, then you need to download it first. It will only show the browsers that you have installed.

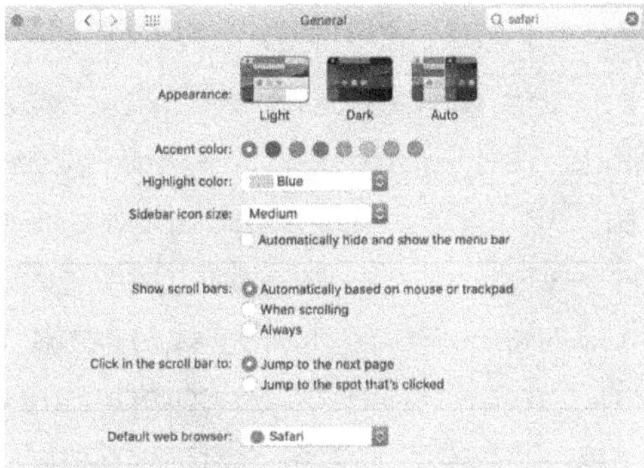

Importing Bookmarks

Starting something new is never fun; if you've been a Chrome or Firefox user, then all those bookmarks you've been collecting for years will not be there.

You can easily move them over, however. Click File > Import From, and select where you want to grab the bookmarks from.

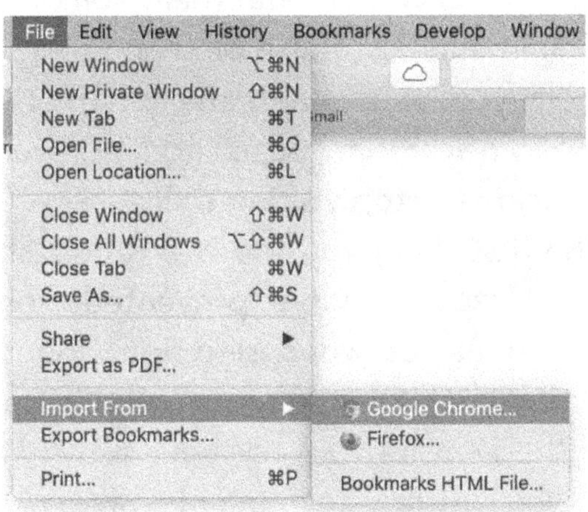

Privacy Report

In an age of frequent security breaches, Apple has taken huge steps to keep your information secure. This is perhaps most apparent in the Privacy Report—a detailed report that tells you what websites see (and don't see) and where your password might have been compromised.

To get started, go to Safari from the menu bar and select Privacy Report.

As the name implies, this is like a report card of websites you visit and not really something that you can go in and customize or change. The goal is just to help you understand the information they are trying to track from you; using that, you may or may not decide to stop visiting them.

The first thing you see is a report showing how many "Trackers" were prevented from following you. You may be wondering right about now "what is a tracker?" A tracker is a little line of code that tells the website to track your activity so it knows who you are (age, gender, browser, location) and what kinds of ads to serve you. If you've ever been on Instagram and saw an ad, then saw that same ad in your browser while reading an article, then saw it several more times on Facebook—it's because they were using trackers to follow you everywhere.

Some people don't really care; some people actually kind of value their privacy. If you fall into that second group, then that's what this report is for.

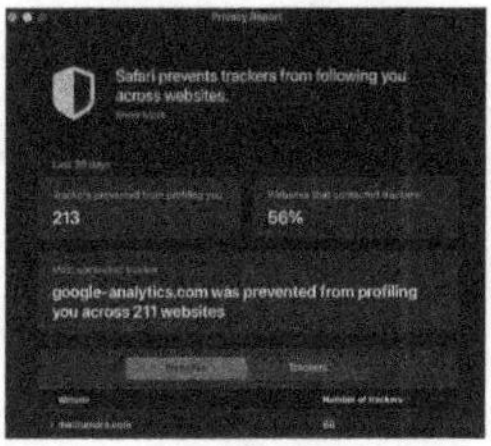

If you drill down further into the website, it will show you all the trackers that they are using.

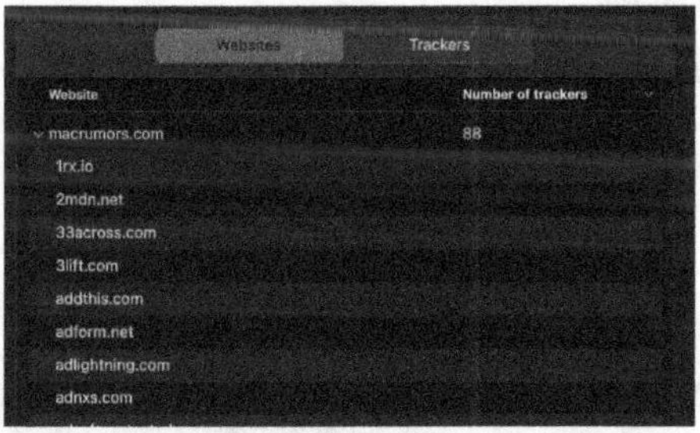

You can also see these trackers by tapping on the tracking icon next to the website address bar and a specific page that you are on.

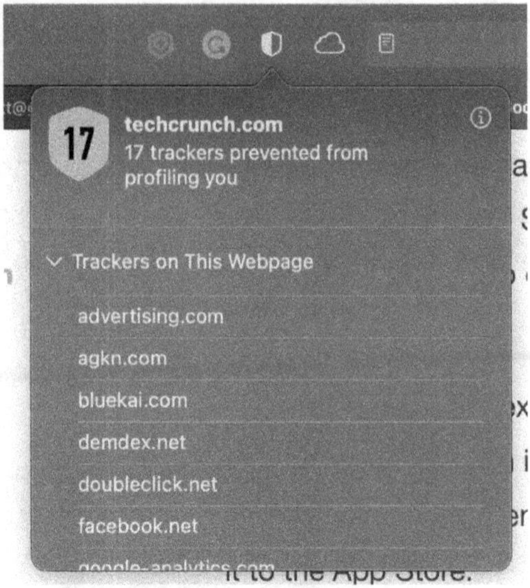

Password Protection

Now that you're paranoid about your privacy, let's look more at how to protect it with password protection.

To get started, go to Safari in the menu bar and select Preference. Then select Passwords from the menu, and make sure "Detect passwords compromised by known data leaks" is checked off.

When you see all the websites load, you'll see some have little ! status triangles. To see what's going on with that website, click it.

Most of them will say one of two things. Either your password "may" have been compromised in a data leak...

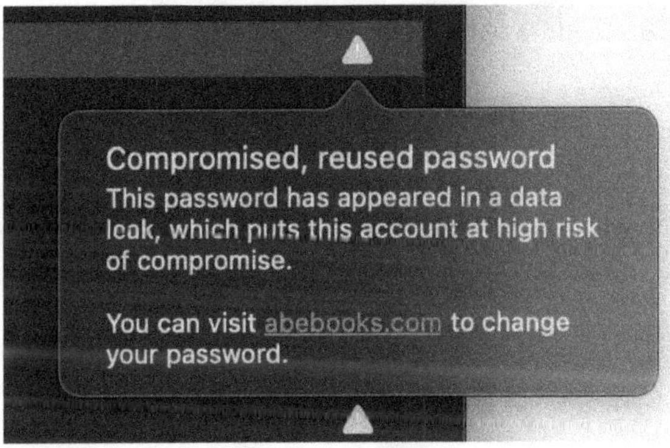

Or your password is weak and easily guessed.

If you are getting the box to change your password, that doesn't absolutely mean you've been hacked. It just means there was a leak and some passwords were compromised.

There are two more areas that will help protect your privacy in the Preference menu. The first is the Privacy tab.

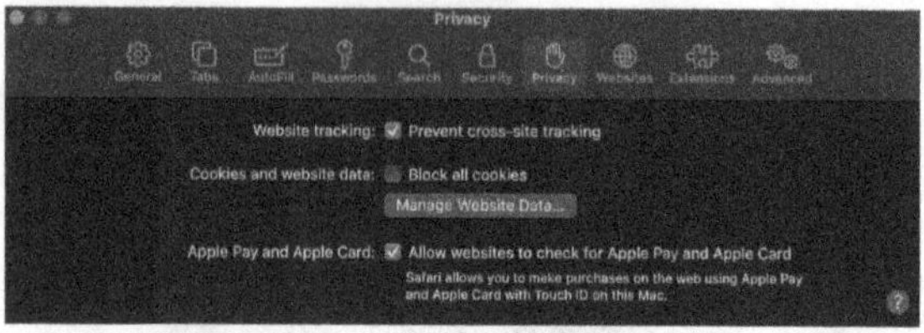

This is where you go if you want to stop those trackers from following you; you can also come here to block all cookies.

The second area is the Security tab. This lets you get a warning when Safari detects a website is not safe and also lets you enable JavaScript.

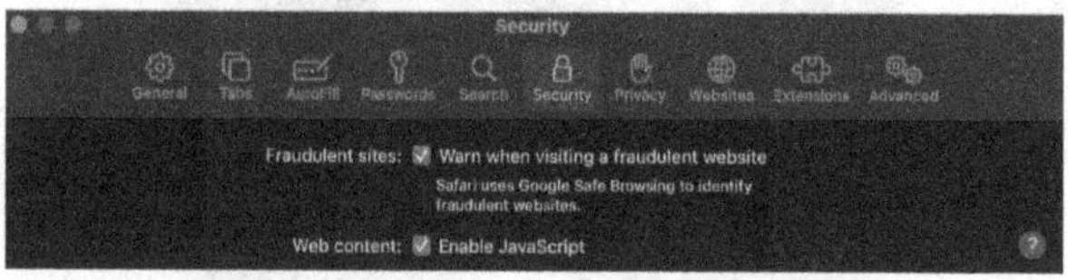

Settings for a Website

When you go to Safari in the menu bar and click Settings for This Website, you will be able to specify specific actions for the website and see what they are able to see.

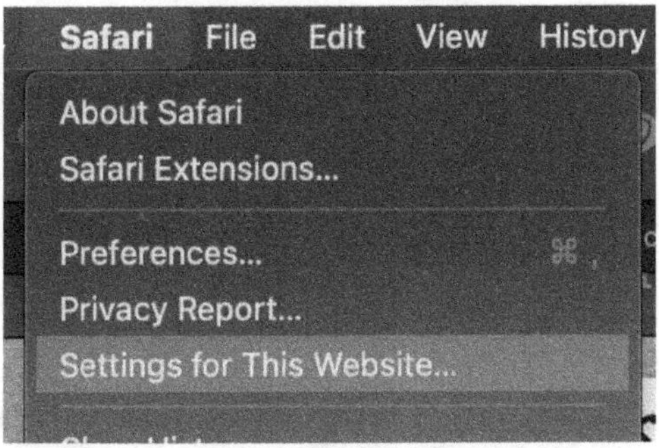

There are only two options you can include on each website: Use Reader when available (this takes away ads and makes the website load sort of like a book) and Enable content blockers (i.e. popups); below this, you can see if they have permission to see things like your camera and microphone.

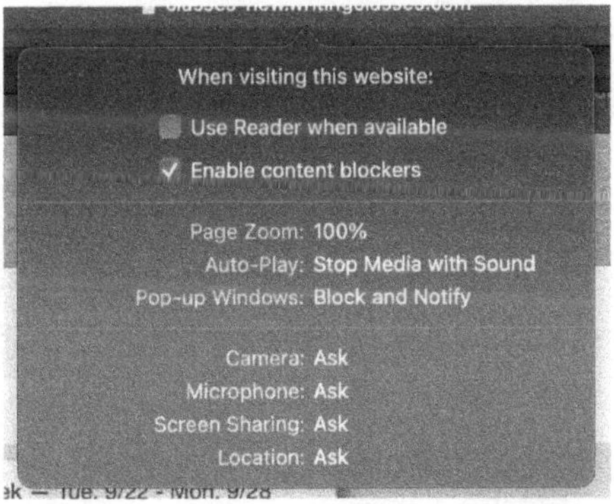

Tab Preview

If you have a lot of tabs open, Safari helps you see what's within a tab with a thumbnail preview. Hover your mouse over your tab, and you'll immediately see a small preview of what is inside that tab.

Translating a Website

One of the newest features to Safari is translations; it's something you've probably used before if you use Chrome. What it does is translates the contents of websites from one language to another. So if a page is in Spanish and you only read English, then you can instantly have the entire page translated.

The process is done by a computer, not a human, so it won't necessarily be the best translation.

To get started, visit a page in another language, then go to View > Translation, then select Translate to English (or whatever language is your default).

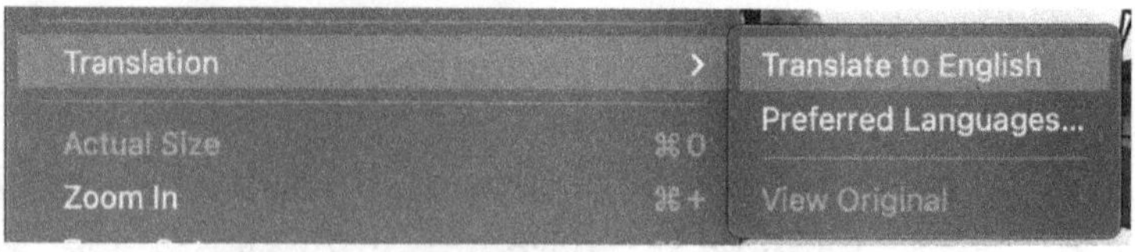

To change your default language, go to Preferred language.

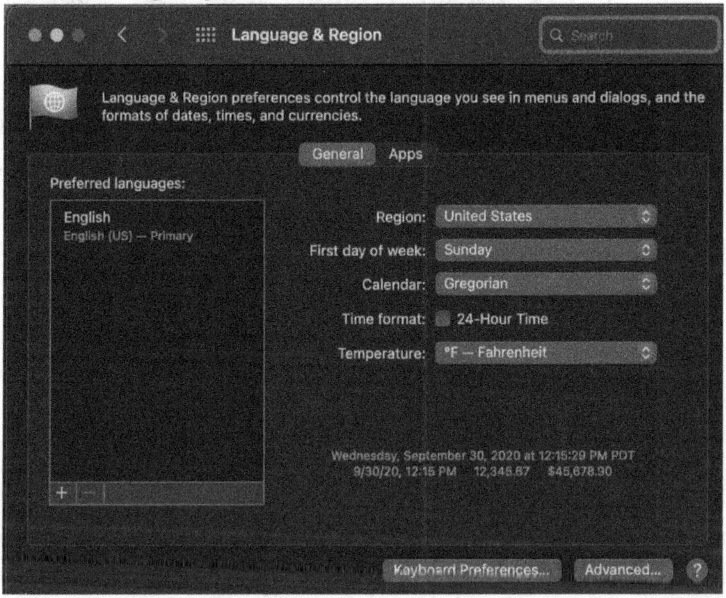

You'll also see an icon appear whenever a website is available to be translated.

Note: while this all may seem very useful, the feature is in beta. If you find it's not accurate, you might want to wait a little bit before trying it again.

Safari for Windows

If you are an iPhone / iPad user trapped in a Windows world, then I have unfortunate news for you: Safari is not for you—at least not on your desktop computer. This guide will still help you with using the browser on your mobile or tablet device running Safari.

Having said that, you can "technically" get Safari for Windows. Several years back, Apple decided to make a stronger push to get the browser in front of more users; they released several versions of Safari for Windows but decided to discontinue it after version 5.

So, while you *cannot* get the current version of Safari on Windows, if you do a Google search for Safari, you will be able to find an older version. My recommendation is not to put Safari on your Windows computer for two reasons: one, it's not supported and what you are downloading is a very old and unstable version; and two, you are downloading it unofficially from other websites so you are opening your computer up to vulnerabilities.

The same is also true if you have an Android phone or Chromebook; there has never been a version of Safari for Chrome OS, but there are plenty of browsers that try and clone the experience. Again, however, my recommendation is to stay away from these; they are from lesser-known companies.

[2]
Safari Extensions

This chapter will cover:

- Finding extensions
- Adding extensions
- Using extensions
- Uninstalling extensions

Extensions extend the capabilities of your browser; think of them like apps for your browser.

Find Extensions

The one unfortunate thing about Safari is that other browsers have a lot more extensions to pick from; the good thing about it, however, is that the ones you find have been vetted and are much better quality.

You can find extensions by clicking on Safari > Safari Extensions.

This opens up the App Store and immediately shows you extensions. You can also search the App Store if you know the extension's name.

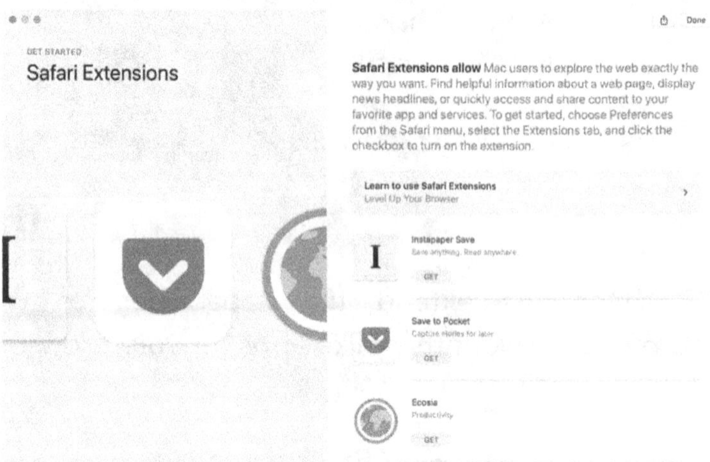

Safari has an area to explain how extensions work and promotes several of them, but don't let this fool you. These are great apps, but there are more extensions than it shows. The best way to see if your favorite extension is available is to search for it. It comes up as any other app, but under the name it will say "Safari Extension."

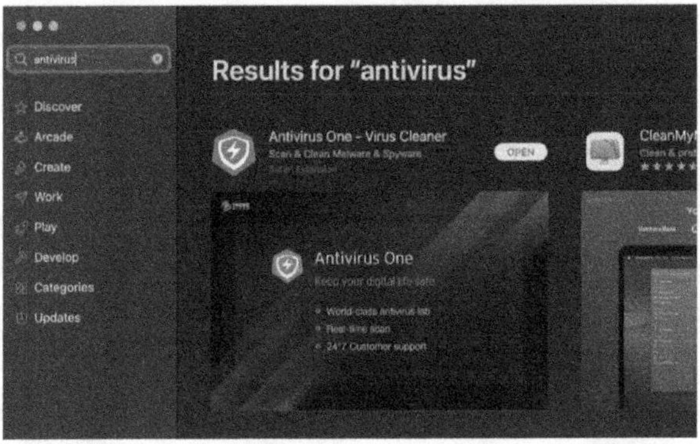

Add an Extension

To add an extension, find the one you want, and then click the blue Get button

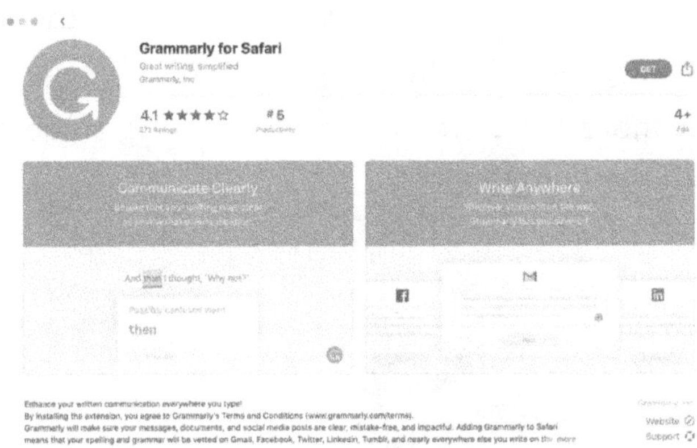

Once it's installed, it will probably give you a popup about allowing notifications. Whatever you pick, you can change it later.

Next, you'll need to go to Safari > Preferences and click the Extensions tab. Find the extension you want to use and check it off.

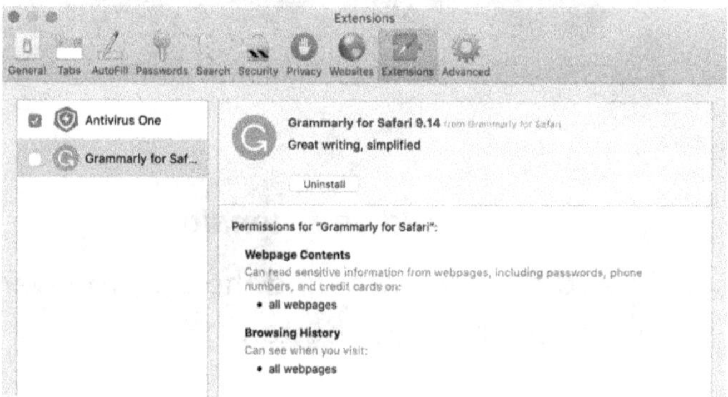

Depending on the extension, there might be a few more extra steps (such as creating an account with the company).

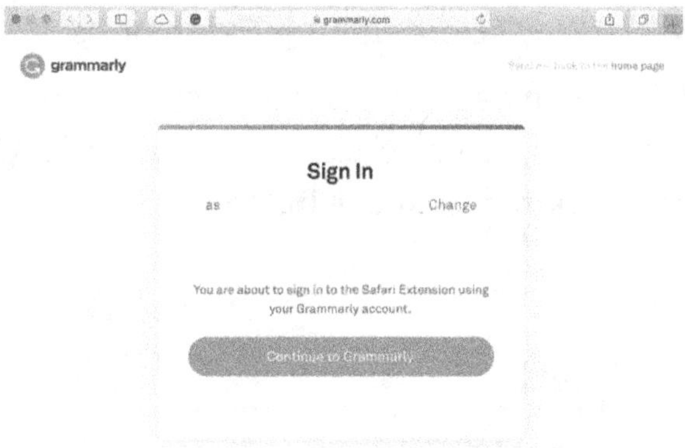

Using Extensions

Some extensions will work behind the scenes and you will rarely notice them; others are more in the foreground.

Earlier in the book, I showed you how to customize the top toolbar; you can refer back to this to add your extension onto the toolbar.

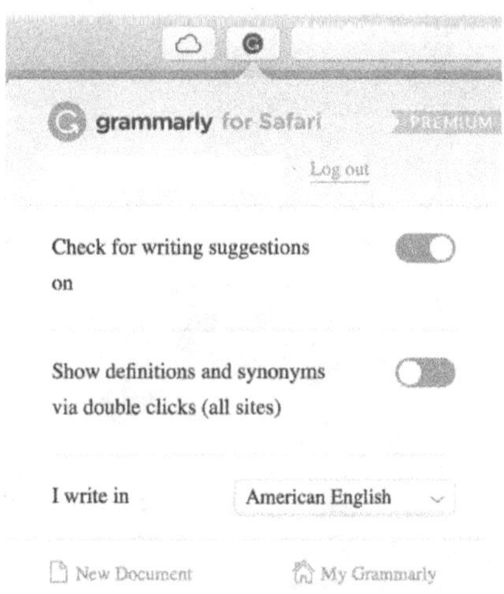

Uninstalling Extensions

To uninstall an extension, go to Safari > Extensions, then click the Extensions tab. From here, click the uninstall button.

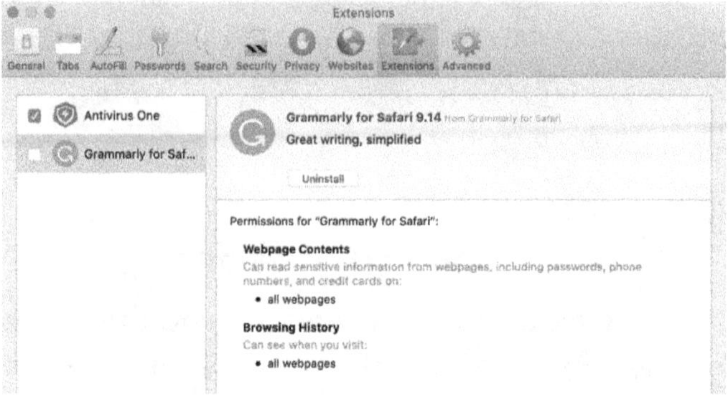

[3]

PRIVACY AND SECURITY

This chapter will cover:

- General Preferences
- Tabs
- AutoFill
- Security
- Privacy

The Preference menu (found by going to Safari > Preferences) contains all the adjustments that you can make within Safari. This section will walk you through what's found in each.

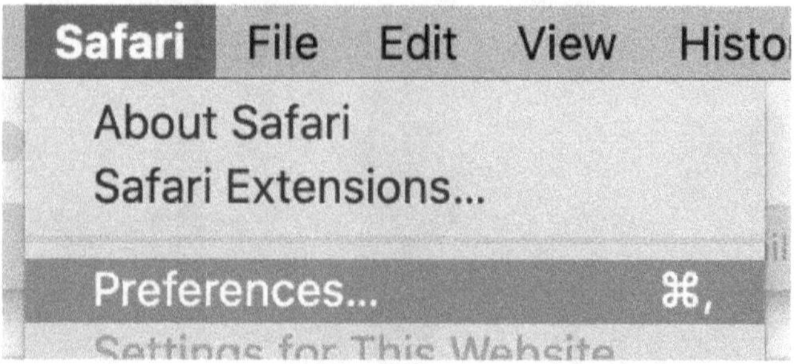

General

General is where you can tell Safari what you want to show when you open the app. When you open a new tab, for example, do you want it to show your favorite websites (the default setting) or something else? You can also tell it where you want downloads to go and when to delete your history.

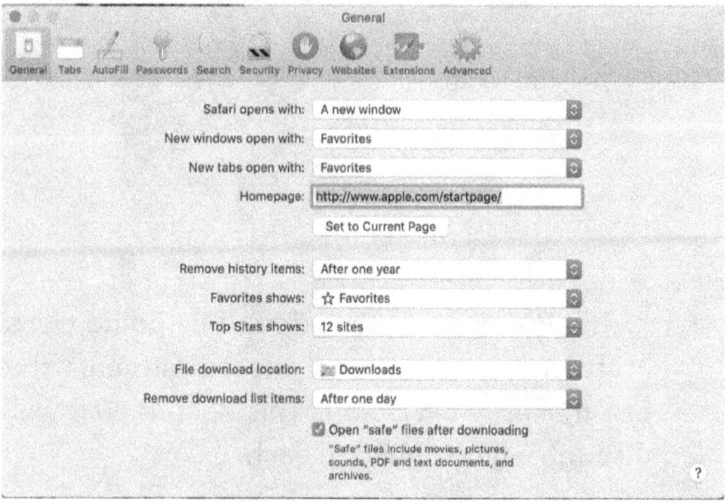

Tabs

There aren't a lot of settings here—just toggles to turn on and off shortcut commands.

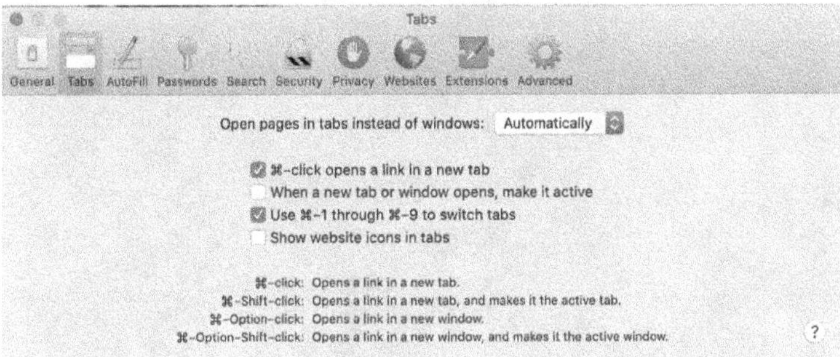

AutoFill

AutoFill is letting Safari remember certain things you type in forms. The setting here you may want to use is "Other Forms." If you click the Edit button, you can remove websites that have your autofill info stored. For example, if you no longer want Safari to remember your username for a particular website, then you can go in here and delete it.

Passwords

Similar to AutoFill, Passwords remembers your passwords for certain websites. So if you decide that you no longer want your password remembered for a shopping website, then you can go in here and delete just that one particular store.

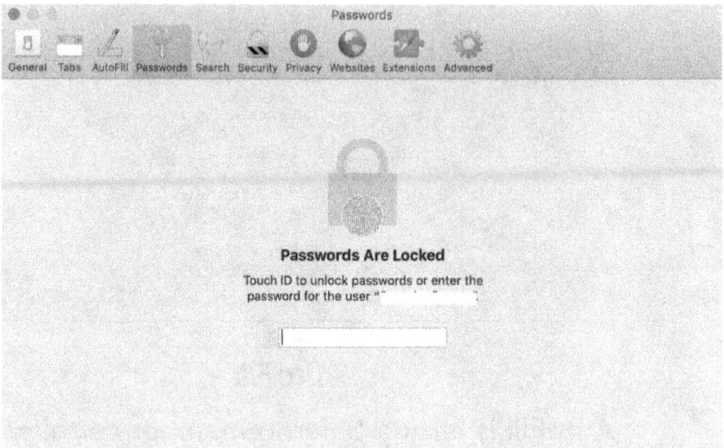

Search

Search lets you change the browser's default search engine (Google) to another search engine—such as Bing, Yahoo, or DuckDuckGo.

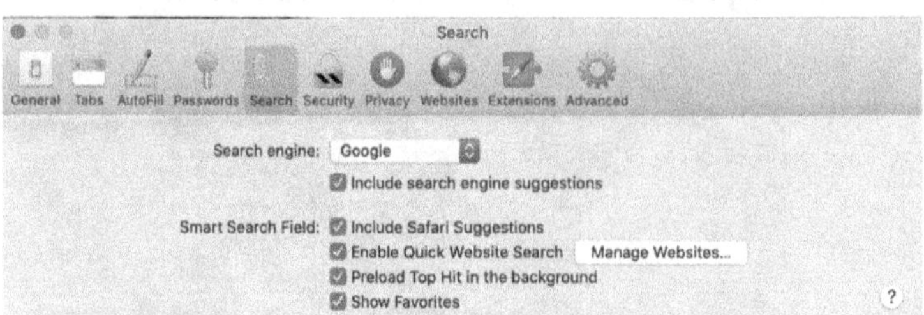

Security

Security is just a very simple toggle menu. By default, both are checked off.

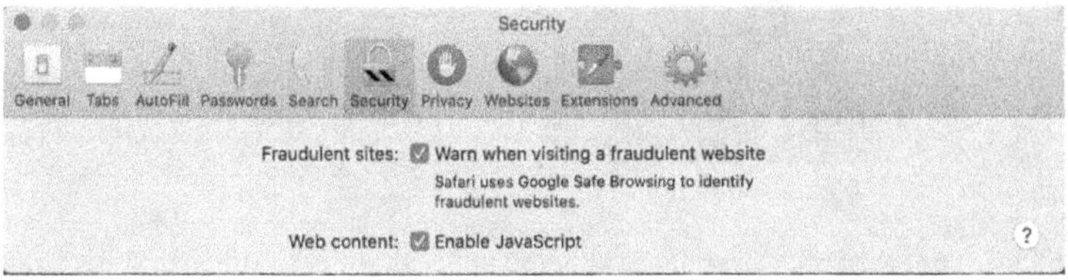

Privacy

Privacy is where you go to turn on and off cookies.

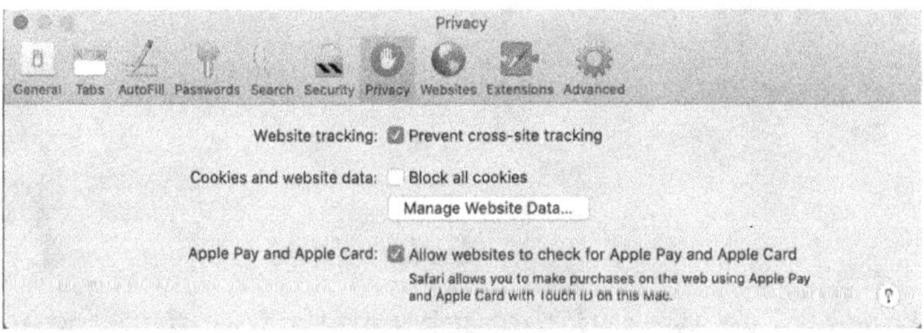

Websites

Websites lets you pick which websites can access certain things on your website. For example, can Facebook access your webcam or can Google maps access your location?

If you ever see those popups that say "Allow or Deny" on your Mac, this is where you can change whatever you picked.

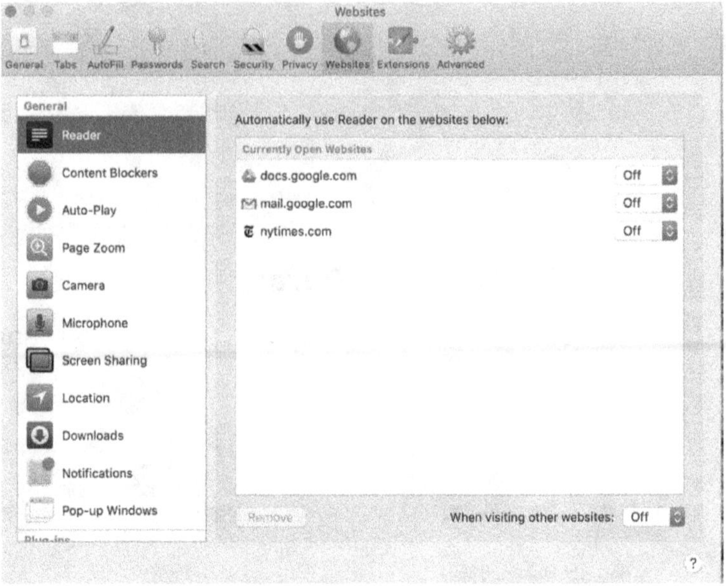

Extensions

I've walked through what's found in Extensions earlier in this book.

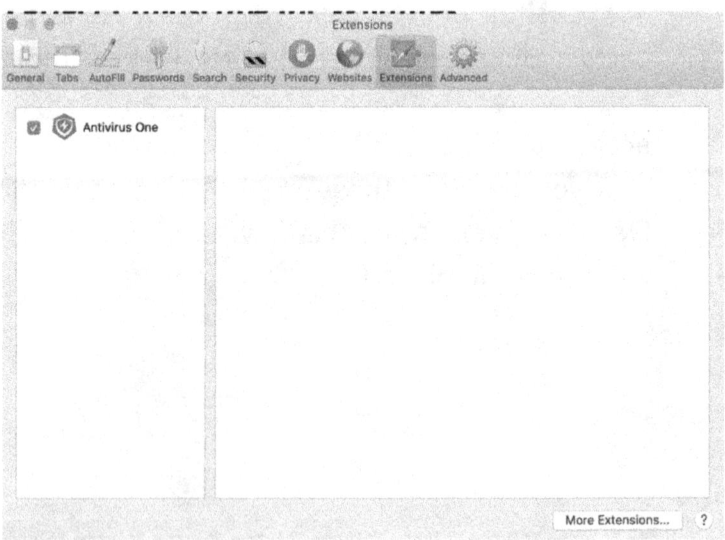

Advanced

Finally, Advanced contains features that you probably will never use (such as encoding).

There is a helpful accessibility section that lets you pick the smallest font size that you will allow.

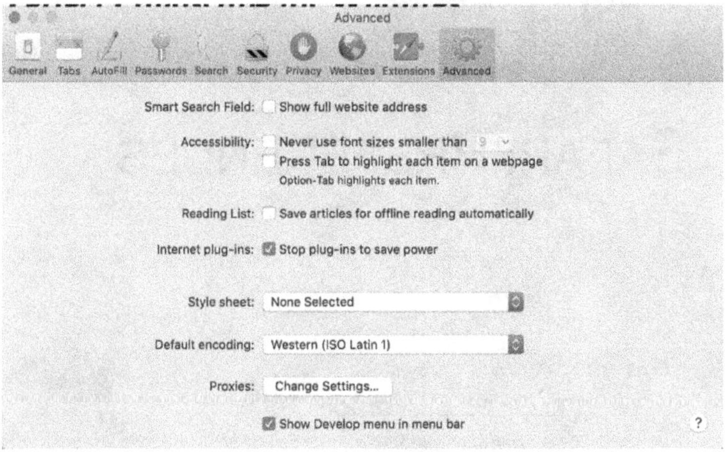

[4]

Safari Preferences

This chapter will cover:

- Password protection
- Firewalls
- Privacy
- Screen time

If your computer is in a place where other people can get to it, or if you are just generally concerned about your privacy being violated, then head on over to Privacy and Security in the System Preferences.

Creating Strong Passwords

Strong passwords are the first line of defense against potential hackers (or smart children!); a strong password is not something like "password"; a strong password has letters, numbers and even symbols in it. It could be something like this: "@mY_MACb00k."

You can use the Password Assistant to test how strong your password is.

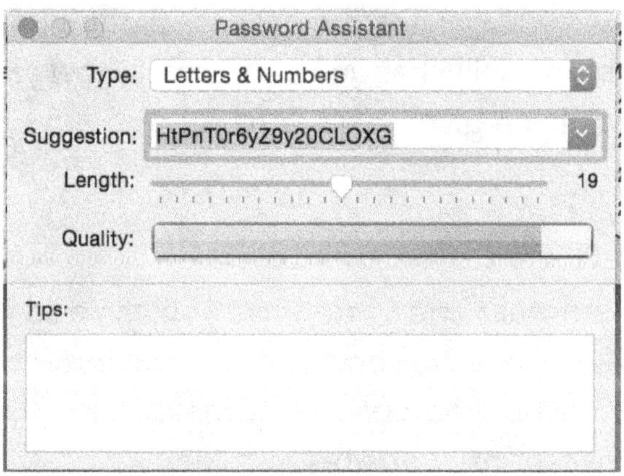

When Keychain loads, you will be able to view the entire list of accounts that are already synced to your Keychain. If you would like to change the password for an account that already exists, find the account and double-click on it. If not, click on the '+' button at the bottom to add a new account.

When the new window comes up, take a look at the bottom. There will be a field for password, and at the right of it will be a small key icon. Click the key icon to open up Password Assistant.

From Type you can select Manual (create your own), Memorable, Letters & Numbers, Numbers Only, Random, and FIPS-181 compliant.

Suggestions will automatically populate, and you can scroll through several different suggestions by using the dropdown menu.

Adjust the length slider to make the password longer or shorter. Any password you create will meet at least these requirements to be considered fair.

As you generate a password, the quality indicator will change to show you how safe and complex a given password is.

Firewall

Another line of defense you can add is a firewall, which protects you from unwanted connections to potentially malicious software applications, websites, or files.

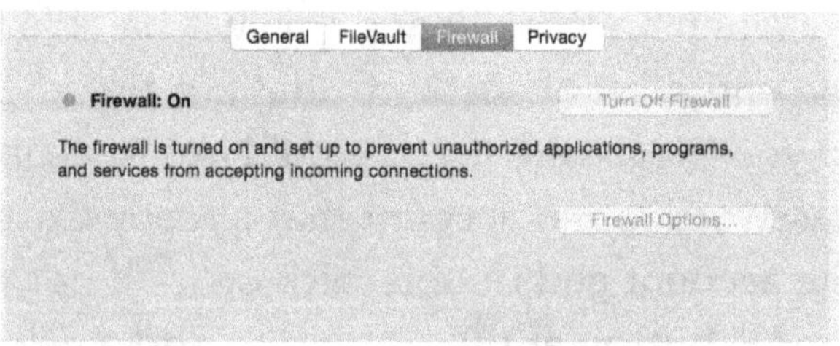

To enable the firewall that comes with your Mac, go to System Preferences > Security & Privacy and select the Firewall tab. Before you can make any changes, click on the lock icon in the bottom left corner and enter your administrator password to continue.

Find My Mac

Just like your iPhone or iPad, Mac comes with a handy feature called "Find My Mac" which lets you find your computer if someone steals it or you misplace it; you can also wipe its hard drive clean remotely.

To enable Find My Mac, go to System Preferences > iCloud and check the box next to Find My Mac. Your location services must also be turned on, so go to System Preferences > Security & Privacy > Privacy > Location Services and make sure Enable Location Services is checked on.

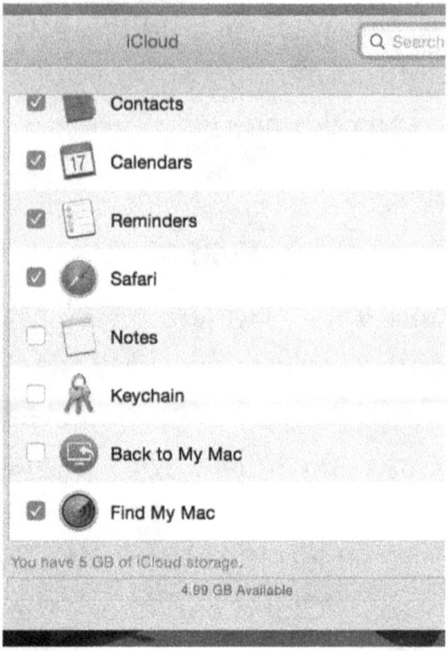

To track your computer, you can log into any computer and visit iCloud.com, enter your iCloud login information, and click on Find My Mac. As long as the Mac is awake and connected to the Internet through Wi-Fi or Ethernet, you will be able to play a loud sound, lock it, or completely erase it so your private information is removed.

Privacy

Apple knows people worry about privacy; they have lots built in to help you control what can (and can't) be seen.

Internet Privacy

If you'd like to clear your search and browsing history, there are two ways to do it: either by clicking on Safari > Clear History and Website Data, or History > Clear History and Website Data. Both can be found on the top menu bar. When the window comes up, you will be able to choose how far back you want the clearing to reach. Once you make a selection, just press the Clear History button to make the changes final.

Cookies allow websites to store data and track certain things, like what other websites you visit during your Internet session, or what kind of products you tend to look at the most. This information is mostly used by advertisers to better target ads for you, but the option is always there if you'd like to disable them. Open up Safari, go to Safari > Preferences, then select the Privacy tab. The cookie options range from allowing all websites to store cookies to blocking all websites. You can also allow cookies only from your most frequently visited websites. If you prefer not to be tracked, check off the box at the bottom that says Ask Websites To Not Track Me. Some websites will not function as you may want them to if you disable this feature.

Application Privacy

The other part of privacy is through installed applications. Go to System Preferences > Security & Privacy and click the Privacy tab. You can shut Location Services off by checking the box next to Enable Location Services. Browse through the left sidebar and you'll be able to customize permissions. If you don't want any apps to access your contacts or calendars, here is where you can block some or all programs from that information.

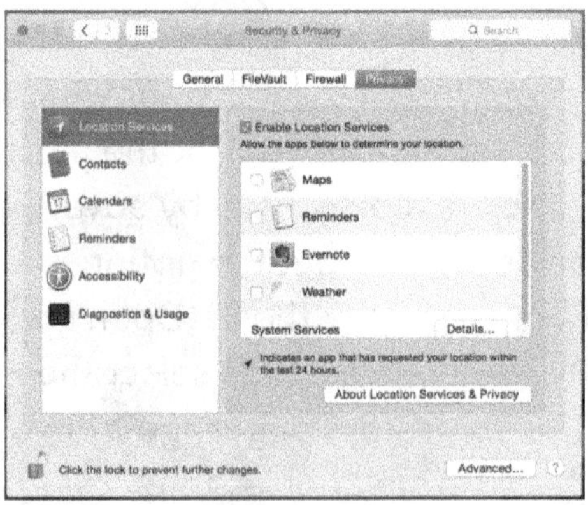

Screen Time

Screen Time might be something you are familiar with. It's been on iPads and iPhones for a while. It came to MacOS with the Catalina update, and is here to stay with Big Sur. What is it? It's a productivity setting that lets you restrict how long you can use certain apps (games for instance). It's highly customizable, so you can set one app like

Word to have zero restrictions, but another one like Internet to have limits.

Screen Time isn't an app in the traditional sense; it's an app within your system settings. To use it, go to System Preferences, then click Screen Time.

This launches a new window that tells you how much time you've been on your computer.

You can set up a passcode by clicking on Options at the bottom of the window.

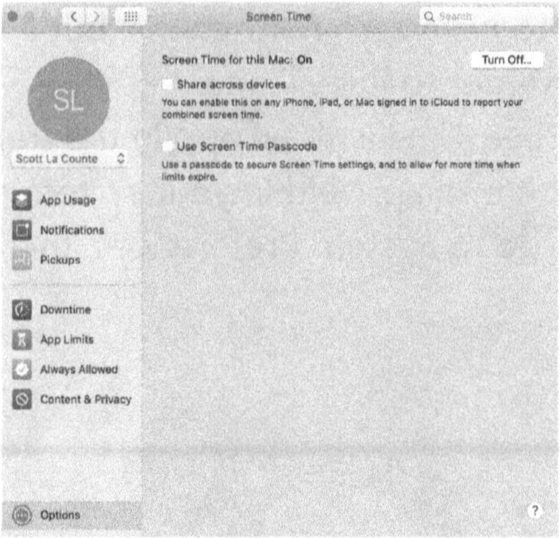

App Limits is where you can start restricting certain apps. Click the '+' in this section.

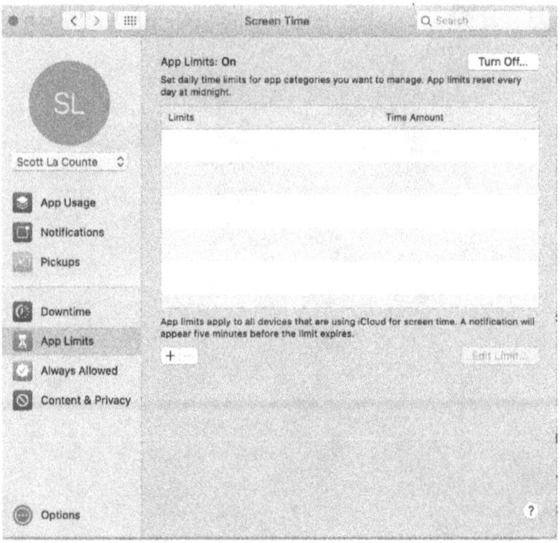

From here, select the app (or kinds of apps) that you want to limit.

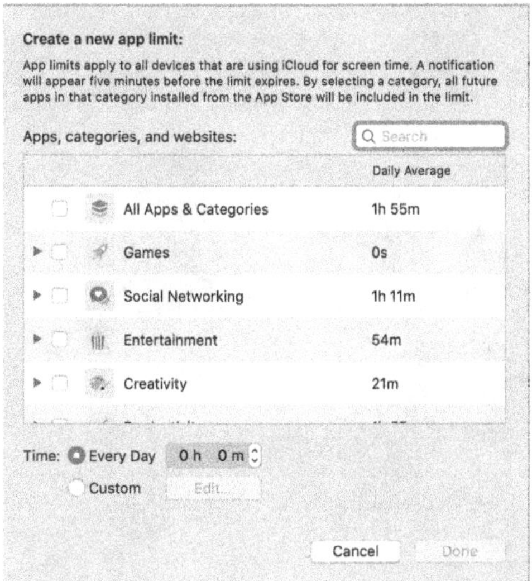

At the bottom, you can say how much time you want to set the limit to.

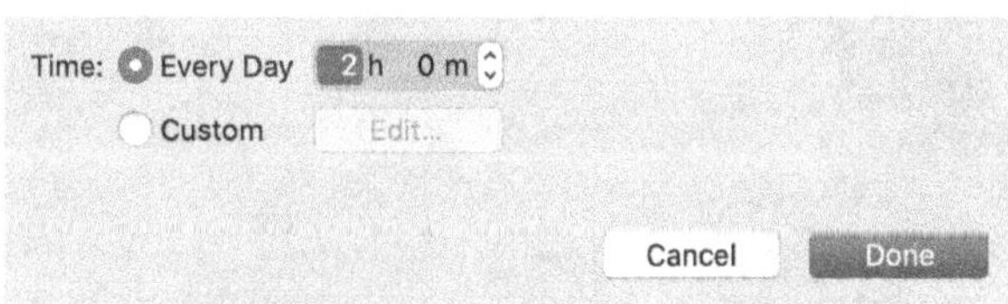

Under Always Allow, you can select apps that have no restrictions.

APPENDIX: KEYBOARD SHORTCUTS

GENERAL SHORTCUTS

Command-X – Cuts or removes selected text or item and copies it to the clipboard.
Command-C – Copies the selected text or item to the clipboard.
Command-V – Pastes the contents of the clipboard into the document, app, or Finder.
Command-Z – Undoes the previous command.
Command- Shift-Z – Redoes the previous undo.
Command-A – Selects all text or items in the running program.
Command-F – Opens the Find window to find documents or other items.
Command-G – Finds the next occurrence of a previously found item (i.e. Find Again).
Command-H – Hides the current running program or front window (Note: this will not work if you have a program running in full screen).
Command-Option-H – Hides all the open apps and windows.

Command-M – Minimizes the currently open window or app (Note: this will not work if you have a program running in full screen).
Command-Option-M – Minimizes all open apps and windows.
Command-N – Opens a new document or window.
Command-O – Opens an item (for instance if you are in Word or Pages and you want to open a previously saved document).
Command-P – Prints the current website or document.
Command-S – Saves the current document.
Command-W – Closes the front window or app
Command-Option-W – Closes all open apps and windows.
Command-Q – Quits an app.
Command-Option-Esc – Force quits a program that is not responding.
Command-Space Bar – Brings up Spotlight to quickly find documents, emails, and apps.
Command-Tab – Switches to the next open app (Note: if you don't let go of Command and continue hitting the Tab button, you can continue going to the next app).
Command-Shift-3 – Takes a screenshot of your entire screen.
Command-, – Opens the Preference menu (if applicable) for the current app.

Document Shortcuts

The following shortcuts are applicable to supported document software like Word, PowerPoint, Pages, Excel, OpenOffice, etc.

Command-B – Bold or un-bold the selected text.
Command-I – Italicize or un-italicize selected text.
Command-U – Underline or remove underline to selected text.

INDEX

ABOUT THE AUTHOR

Scott La Counte is a librarian and writer. His first book, *Quiet, Please: Dispatches from a Public Librarian* (Da Capo 2008) was the editor's choice for the Chicago Tribune and a Discovery title for the Los Angeles Times; in 2011, he published the YA book The N00b Warriors, which became a #1 Amazon bestseller; his most recent book is *#OrganicJesus: Finding Your Way to an Unprocessed, GMO-Free Christianity* (Kregel 2016).

He has written dozens of best-selling how-to guides on tech products.

You can connect with him at ScottDouglas.org.